PROPELLING INNOVATION

PROPELLING INNOVATION

The Jet Propulsion Secrets of Squid

SAM LORAY

CONTENTS

INDEX

INTRODUCTION

The normal world has for some time been a wellspring of motivation for human development, offering a gold mine of answers for complex difficulties. Among the bunch wonders of nature, the modest squid arises as an improbable yet charming dream for researchers and architects. Squid, with their strange and proficient stream drive frameworks, have caught the creative mind of analysts trying to disentangle the privileged insights of their submerged velocity. This investigation into the stream drive privileged insights of squid not just uncovers the unpredictable biomechanics of these cephalopods yet additionally impels a rush of development across different mechanical spaces.

In the huge territory of the world's seas, squid explore with unrivaled beauty, easily skimming through water with an impetus component that has developed more than great many years. The drive arrangement of squid, established in the withdrawal of their strong mantle and the removal of water, remains as a demonstration of the marvels of normal designing. As researchers dig into the subtleties of this component, they uncover rules that rise above the marine domain, igniting development in fields as different as advanced mechanics, aviation design, and clinical gadgets.

This excursion into the fly drive privileged insights of squid fills in as a microcosm of the more extensive pattern of biomimicry — a discipline that looks for motivation from nature to address human difficulties. The standards drawn from the investigation of squid impetus improve how we might interpret sea life science as well as proposition a plan for planning innovations that are productive, versatile, and supportable. This investigation isn't restricted to the research center; it resounds with a significant association between the regular world and the human journey for information and progress.

Disclosing the Puzzle: Squid and Their Stream Drive System

1. **The Cephalopod Odyssey**
   Prior to diving into the complexities of squid drive, it is fundamental to set

out on a concise investigation of cephalopods — the surprising class of marine creatures that incorporates squid, octopuses, and cuttlefish. Cephalopods are portrayed by their unmistakable morphology, with noticeable limbs, a nose like mouth, and profoundly created knowledge. These marine wonders occupy various maritime conditions, from shallow waterfront waters to the deep profundities, exhibiting surprising flexibility.

Squid, inside the cephalopod family, stand apart for their stream drive capacities. Dissimilar to fish that depend on balance developments for impetus, squid utilize an interesting system based on the constriction of their mantle — a strong construction that encompasses their bodies. This withdrawal removes water strongly, producing a strong fly that impels the squid forward. The polish and productivity of this impetus framework have captivated researchers and made way for a more profound investigation into its biomechanical complexities.

2. **Stream Impetus Divulged**

The stream impetus instrument of squid is a wonder of transformative variation, finely tuned for their maritime way of life. At the core of this framework is the mantle, a solid organ that envelopes the instinctive mass of the squid. As the mantle contracts, water inside the mantle cavity is ousted through a siphon, making a powerful fly. The course of the fly is constrained by the direction of the siphon, permitting squid to explore with striking deftness.

This impetus strategy offers a few benefits in the submerged climate. Dissimilar to balance based drive, stream impetus takes into account fast speed increase and deceleration, empowering squid to quickly dodge hunters or seek after prey. Moreover, the shortfall of inflexible balances diminishes hydrodynamic drag, improving the general proficiency of development. The stream impetus framework embodies the style of nature's answers for the difficulties of movement in a liquid medium.

3. **Biomechanics of Squid Impetus**

The biomechanics of squid drive include a mind boggling interchange of strong compressions, liquid elements, and hydrodynamics. The mantle muscles, comprising of roundabout and spiral strands, work in coordination to produce the fundamental power for water removal. The shape and adaptability of the mantle add to the productivity of the stream, considering exact control of course and speed.

Liquid elements assume a pivotal part in the drive cycle. As the mantle contracts, water is quickly brought into the mantle depression. The conclusion of the mantle gap seals the hole, and the constriction of muscles removes the water through the siphon. This removal creates a push that impels the squid the other way. The effectiveness of this instrument is a consequence of the complicated coordination of strong activities and hydrodynamic standards.

Biomimicry: Drawing Motivation from Nature's Playbook

1. **Biomimicry as an Impetus for Development**

   The investigation of nature's plans and cycles has long propelled human creativity. Biomimicry, a discipline established in drawing motivation from the normal world, has arisen as an impetus for development across different fields. By copying the effectiveness, flexibility, and maintainability saw in organic frameworks, researchers and designers mean to address complex difficulties and advance mechanical arrangements.

   The stream drive insider facts of squid address an enamoring passage point into the immense domain of biomimicry. The standards overseeing squid headway offer a worldview for planning drive frameworks that rise above the limits of ordinary designing. As specialists disentangle the complexities of squid biomechanics, they end up at the convergence of science and innovation, ready to move advancement in unanticipated headings.

2. **Squid Biomimicry: A Mechanical Odyssey**

   The use of squid biomimicry stretches out a long ways past the interest of grasping marine motion. It makes ready for extraordinary mechanical headways with expected applications in fields going from advanced mechanics to aeronautic design. The standards gathered from squid drive act as building blocks for the plan of productive and nimble frameworks that can explore complex conditions.

   In the domain of mechanical technology, squid-roused plans have led to submerged vehicles referred to casually as "squid-bots." These robots, furnished with biomimetic drive frameworks, show a degree of mobility and proficiency beforehand impossible. As they coast through submerged scenes, these soft robots represent the combination of organic motivation and mechanical development, offering experiences into the fate of independent oceanic investigation.

3. **Advanced plane design Takes Off**

   The standards of squid drive track down reverberation in the endless skies, as aviation design specialists investigate the coordination of biomimetic plans into airplane impetus frameworks. The conventional strategies for fly drive, motivated by the smoothed out effectiveness of bird flight, are presently supplemented by bits of knowledge from the sea profundities. Squid-roused impetus frameworks can possibly reform airplane configuration, offering options that are productive as well as versatile to fluctuating flight conditions.

   Envision airplane that can change their drive instruments in light of the standards of squid velocity — quick speed increase, exact control, and negligible energy use. The marriage of nature's creativity with human designing ability opens roads for airplane that mirror the elegance and effectiveness of marine cephalopods, proclaiming another time in aviation advancement.

4. **Clinical Gadgets Mellowed Naturally**

Past the domains of mechanical technology and aviation, squid biomimicry penetrates the field of clinical gadgets and delicate advanced mechanics. The adaptability and accuracy of the squid's fly drive framework act as an outline for the improvement of delicate, versatile mechanical gadgets. These gadgets, propelled by the flexible developments of squid arms, hold massive potential for insignificantly obtrusive operations.

Picture a careful robot, directed by standards got from the squid's mantle compression, exploring with accuracy through mind boggling physical designs. The biomimetic approach improves the usefulness of these gadgets as well as adds to the advancement of additional patient-accommodating and flexible clinical innovations. The combination of science and designing in this setting represents the expansive effect of biomimicry on human prosperity.

From Sea Profundities to Advancement Levels: The Meaning of Squid Biomimicry

1. **Natural Meaning of Squid Drive**
   Before we dive further into the mechanical ramifications of squid biomimicry, appreciating the biological meaning of squid impetus right at home is significant. Squid, as dynamic hunters and prey, assume a fundamental part in marine biological systems. Their capacity to quickly explore the sea permits them to take part in complex ways of behaving like hunting, getting away from hunters, and mating.
   The effectiveness of squid drive isn't exclusively a wonder of biomechanical designing; it is a step by step process for surviving finely tuned by development. Squid, through their fly drive, encapsulate a unique relationship with their current circumstance, impacting hunter prey elements and adding to the general equilibrium of marine biological systems. Understanding the natural setting of squid motion adds layers of intricacy to the story, featuring the interconnectedness of organic variations and ecological elements.

2. **Mechanical Interpretation: Squid Biomimicry in real life**
   The interpretation of squid biomimicry into mechanical development requires a nuanced comprehension of the fundamental standards. As analysts unravel the biomechanics of squid drive, they face the test of refining complex organic cycles into commonsense designing arrangements. This cycle includes not just duplicating the actual parts of squid velocity yet additionally catching the pith of effectiveness, versatility, and manageability innate in the normal framework.
   In the domain of mechanical technology, the interpretation is clear in the advancement of submerged vehicles that mirror the squid's impetus framework. These vehicles, furnished with adaptable materials and biomimetic impetus components, explore submerged conditions with a degree of accuracy that reflects their natural partners. The reconciliation of man-made consciousness further upgrades the versatility of these soft robots, permitting them to answer

natural signs and explore testing landscapes independently.

Plane design specialists make an interpretation of squid biomimicry into creative airplane plans, where the standards of stream drive track down applications in impetus frameworks that go past customary motors. The reception of adaptable materials and dynamic impetus systems empowers airplane to copy the coordinated developments of squid in water. This interpretation reaches out to clinical gadgets, where the delicate and adaptable nature of squid-motivated mechanical technology works with insignificantly obtrusive methodology, diminishing the effect on patients and working on careful results.

3. **Preservation Suggestions**

The crossing point of mechanical development and the normal world delivers moral contemplations, especially with regards to preservation. As analysts draw motivation from squid impetus to foster state of the art innovations, it becomes basic to guarantee that these undertakings line up with standards of natural stewardship. The protection ramifications of squid biomimicry stretch out to both the marine biological systems that squids possess and the more extensive environmental scene.

Mindful biomimicry includes a promise to reasonable practices, moral obtaining of materials, and a careful comprehension of the likely natural effects of innovative applications. The preservation of squid populaces, alongside other marine species, becomes interlaced with the moral quest for advancement. This combination of moral contemplations highlights the significance of an all encompassing methodology that thinks about the advantages of innovative progression as well as its natural impression.

The Odyssey Keeps: Investigating Unfamiliar Regions

1. **Past Squid: Investigating Assorted Biomes**
   While squid biomimicry offers an enthralling section point into the universe of biomimetic development, the odyssey of investigation reaches out past cephalopods. Nature, in its monstrous variety, gives a rich embroidery of motivation drawn from different biomes, environments, and species. From the infinitesimal universe of microscopic organisms to the transcending overhangs of rainforests, every living space harbors special variations that can possibly shape the fate of innovation.

   The investigation of unfamiliar domains includes a multidisciplinary approach, uniting researcher, specialists, environmentalists, and materials researchers. The mission for motivation traverses earthbound and oceanic conditions, opening the mysteries of organic entities that have advanced to flourish in outrageous circumstances, tackle sunlight based energy with proficiency, or explore complex scenes with accuracy.

2. **Environmental Change as an Impetus for Investigation**

The criticalness of tending to worldwide difficulties, especially the effects of environmental change, fills in as an impetus for investigation and development. Nature-roused arrangements become a wellspring of innovative progression as well as a vital methodology for moderating and adjusting to the evolving environment. From the strength of mangrove environments to the energy-productive methodologies of desert-abiding organic entities, the investigation of assorted biomes offers bits of knowledge into procedures for environment versatility.

The joining of environmental change contemplations into biomimetic research lines up with the more extensive ethos of manageability. As analysts explore the intricacies of environment driven difficulties, the illustrations drawn from nature's flexibility become essential to creating methodologies that advance ecological preservation and variation.

1. Definition of Innovation

Development, a term universal in present day talk, exemplifies the substance of human imagination and progress. It rises above enterprises, trains, and societies, filling in as a main impetus behind cultural headways. As we leave on an investigation of the multi-layered elements of advancement, we unwind its definition, inspecting the complexities that characterize this dynamic and groundbreaking idea.

The Pith of Advancement

1. **Characterizing Development**
   At its center, development addresses the most common way of presenting clever thoughts, techniques, items, or administrations that outcome in significant and positive change. It reaches out past simple development, incorporating the execution and reception of savvy fixes that address existing difficulties or satisfy neglected needs. Development, hence, is a dynamic and iterative cycle that drives social orders forward by encouraging nonstop improvement and variation.

2. **The Interchange of Imagination and Application**
   Inventiveness comprises the central flash of development. It includes the age of unique and important thoughts, frequently determined by an oddity to investigate strange domains. Be that as it may, development separates itself through the realistic utilization of innovative thoughts. It includes changing theoretical ideas into unmistakable arrangements that have a certifiable effect. This interchange of innovativeness and application leads to the unique idea of development, as it explores the scaffold among creative mind and reasonableness.

3. **Various Appearances of Development**
   Development appears in different structures, going from gradual enhancements to weighty outlook changes. It tends to be item arranged, as found in the advancement of new advancements or purchaser products, or cycle situated,

improving existing strategies to upgrade productivity. Besides, advancement reaches out into authoritative designs, plans of action, and social structures, forming the manner in which we live, work, and communicate.

4. **The Job of Innovation in Advancement**

In the contemporary scene, innovation assumes a urgent part in driving development. The fast headways in computerized advancements, man-made consciousness, and network have introduced a period where mechanical development saturates virtually every aspect of human existence. This mechanical development speeds up the speed of advancement as well as makes additional opportunities and difficulties that request intelligent fixes.

Kinds of Advancement

1. **Steady versus Problematic Advancement**
   Advancement can be grouped into two general classes: steady and problematic. Steady development includes progressive and consistent upgrades to existing items, administrations, or cycles. It frequently centers around improving effectiveness, decreasing expenses, or refining client encounters. Troublesome development, then again, presents extremist and extraordinary changes that can reshape whole businesses. It challenges laid out standards, frequently delivering existing arrangements out of date.

2. **Open and Shut Development**
   The cooperative idea of development recognizes open and shut advancement models. Shut advancement includes inner innovative work inside an association, depending on in-house mastery to drive development. Open development, conversely, embraces outer coordinated effort, taking advantage of outside information, thoughts, and assets. It perceives that significant bits of knowledge might exist past hierarchical limits, empowering associations, and coordinated effort with outer elements.

3. **Social Development**
   Past the domain of items and advances, social development tends to cultural difficulties, intending to further develop the prosperity of networks. It includes the improvement of new answers for social issues like destitution, disparity, and natural supportability. Social development frequently arises through cooperative endeavors that influence assorted viewpoints and disciplines to make positive cultural effect.

4. **Maintainable Development**

With a developing consciousness of ecological difficulties, feasible advancement centers around making arrangements that offset monetary suitability with natural and social obligation. It includes eco-accommodating practices, sustainable power innovations, and round economy models that limit squander and advance long haul natural manageability.

The Development Interaction

1. **Distinguishing proof of Chances**

   The development interaction starts with the distinguishing proof of chances or difficulties that warrant intelligent fixes. This stage includes cautious perception, market investigation, and a comprehension of client needs. Pioneers try to reveal neglected requests or regions where enhancements can be made.

2. **Thought Age**

   Whenever potential open doors are recognized, the subsequent stage includes creating thoughts. This stage embraces unique reasoning, empowering a huge number of inventive ideas without prompt requirements. Procedures, for example, conceptualizing, mind planning, and configuration believing are usually utilized to animate ideation.

3. **Assessment and Determination**

   Not all thoughts produced during the ideation stage are practical or lined up with hierarchical objectives. The assessment and determination process includes examining potential arrangements in light of measures, for example, practicality, market interest, and arrangement with key targets. Pioneers should arrive at informed conclusions about which thoughts to seek after further.

4. **Advancement and Prototyping**

   The picked thoughts progress to the improvement stage, where ideas are changed into substantial models or least feasible items. This stage includes iterative testing and refinement to guarantee that the proposed arrangements satisfy quality guidelines and client assumptions.

5. **Execution**

   Fruitful advancement comes full circle in the execution stage, where refined arrangements are acquainted with the market or coordinated into hierarchical cycles. Execution requires powerful undertaking the board, coordinated effort, and an essential way to deal with explore likely difficulties and guarantee a smooth progress from idea to the real world.

6. **Assessment and Cycle**

The advancement interaction is recurrent instead of direct. Following execution, progressing assessment is fundamental to evaluate the effect of developments and distinguish regions for development. Input from clients, market elements, and innovative progressions might incite further cycles or the improvement of completely new arrangements.

The Drivers of Development

1. **Interest and Investigation**
   Development frequently springs from an inborn interest to investigate the unexplored world. Inquisitive personalities question business as usual, look for new points of view, and are available to capricious thoughts. The quest for information, combined with an eagerness to wander into unknown regions, shapes the establishment for extraordinary development.

2. **Cross-Disciplinary Cooperation**
   In an interconnected world, cross-disciplinary cooperation powers advancement by uniting people with assorted ability. Cooperative endeavors that range disciplines, enterprises, and societies encourage a rich trade of thoughts, viewpoints, and techniques. The combination of various information spaces frequently brings about imaginative arrangements that rise above customary limits.

3. **Business and Chance Taking**
   Business is firmly entwined with advancement, as it implies the readiness to face challenges and seek after clever open doors. Trailblazers and business people share a typical quality — the capacity to explore vulnerability, embrace carefully thought out plans of action, and persevere notwithstanding difficulties. Risk-taking turns into an impetus for cutting edge developments that can possibly rethink businesses.

4. **Innovative Headways**

The fast development of innovation fills in as both a driver and an empowering influence of advancement. Progressions in figuring power, availability, man-made reasoning, and materials science make additional opportunities and roads for investigation. Innovation driven development speeds up the speed of progress, reforming enterprises and forming the direction of cultural advancement.

Provokes and Hindrances to Advancement

1. **Protection from Change**
   Intrinsic protection from change represents a huge boundary to development. People and associations, alright with laid out schedules and cycles, might be hesitant to embrace novel thoughts or leave from recognizable practices. Beating opposition requires successful correspondence, initiative, and an essential way to deal with oversee changes.

2. **Asset Limitations**
   Advancement frequently requests assets, including monetary venture, ability, and time. Associations confronting asset limitations might find it trying to apportion the vital assets for innovative work. Adjusting the requirement for development with monetary real factors turns into a sensitive yet vital part of driving economical advancement.

3. **Absence of Cooperation**
   Storehouses inside associations and restricted cooperation between various elements prevent the free progression of thoughts and different points of view. Development blossoms with cooperation, and separating obstructions between offices, ventures, and scholarly establishments encourages a more helpful climate for innovative ideation and critical thinking.

4. **Apprehension about Disappointment**

The apprehension about disappointment can deaden advancement endeavors. People or associations reluctant to embrace disappointment as an innate piece of the advancement cycle might try not to face challenges. Notwithstanding, disappointment frequently gives important examples and bits of knowledge that add to future achievement. Moving the viewpoint on disappointment as a venturing stone to development is fundamental for cultivating a culture of consistent improvement.

The Fate of Advancement

1. **Arising Patterns**
   A few arising patterns shape the future scene of development. Man-made consciousness and AI, for example, are ready to alter different enterprises, mechanizing processes and enlarging human capacities. Furthermore, the intermingling of advances, like the Web of Things, blockchain, and 5G network, opens new outskirts for imaginative arrangements that influence interconnected environments.

2. **Moral Contemplations**
   As development advances, moral contemplations become progressively urgent. Trailblazers and associations should explore the moral ramifications of their manifestations, taking into account issues like information security, social effect, and ecological supportability. Adjusting the quest for development with moral obligation guarantees that innovative progressions contribute emphatically to society.

3. **Worldwide Cooperation**
   The interconnected idea of worldwide difficulties, for example, environmental change, medical services, and financial disparity, highlights the significance of worldwide coordinated effort in driving significant advancement. Cooperative drives that include different partners, including legislatures, organizations, the scholarly community, and non-benefit associations, intensify the aggregate effect of development on a worldwide scale.

4. **Human-Focused Development**

Human-focused plan standards place the end-client at the center of the development cycle. Understanding client needs, inclinations, and encounters becomes key to making arrangements that resound with individuals. The eventual fate of development is progressively described by an emphasis on improving the prosperity and fulfillment of people, guaranteeing that mechanical headways line up with human qualities.

B. Importance of Innovation in Various Industries

Development remains as the backbone of progress, driving positive changes across different enterprises. The significance of development couldn't possibly be more significant, as it powers monetary development as well as addresses complex difficulties, upgrades intensity, and cultivates a culture of persistent improvement. In this investigation, we dig into the significant job of development across different areas, enlightening its expansive effect on ventures that shape the advanced world.

1. **Innovation and Data Innovation (IT) Industry**

   Driving Innovative Progressions

   The innovation and IT industry exemplifies the advantageous connection among advancement and progress. Steady advancement is the standard in this unique area, where organizations competition to foster state of the art arrangements that reclassify how people and organizations cooperate with innovation. From the appearance of PCs to the period of distributed computing and man-made reasoning, advancement moves the business forward, driving productivity, network, and the development of computerized environments.

   Empowering Advanced Change

   Development is the main impetus behind computerized change, an essential basic for associations looking to remain pertinent in the computerized age. Advancements like the Web of Things (IoT), blockchain, and AI are reshaping plans of action, smoothing out tasks, and making new roads for esteem creation. The capacity to adjust and coordinate imaginative arrangements has turned into a critical differentiator for organizations in the innovation and IT scene.

   Network protection Headways

   As innovation propels, so do the difficulties connected with network protection. Advancement assumes a pivotal part in creating vigorous network protection arrangements that shield information and computerized foundation. From cutting edge encryption calculations to modern danger recognition frameworks, nonstop development is fundamental for stay in front of digital dangers and safeguard the respectability of advanced environments.

2. **Medical care Industry**

   Clinical Leap forwards and Treatment Modalities

   Development in the medical services industry straightforwardly affects human prosperity, driving progressions in clinical therapies, diagnostics, and patient consideration. Leap forwards in biotechnology, genomics, and customized medication have changed the comprehension and treatment of sicknesses. Accuracy medication, empowered by inventive advancements, tailors clinical intercessions to individual hereditary profiles, streamlining helpful results and limiting aftereffects.

Telemedicine and Far off Quiet Consideration

Ongoing years have seen a flood in imaginative answers for far off tolerant consideration and telemedicine. Advanced wellbeing stages, wearable gadgets, and telehealth applications influence innovation to give open and advantageous medical care administrations. These advancements upgrade patient comfort as well as add to the improvement of medical care assets and the conveyance of opportune clinical mediations.

Wellbeing Informatics and Information Investigation

The reconciliation of wellbeing informatics and information examination embodies how advancement changes medical care conveyance. Electronic wellbeing records, information driven experiences, and prescient examination engage medical care experts to go with informed choices, improve patient results, and smooth out medical services tasks. The intermingling of innovation and medical care is making an information driven environment that holds the possibility to reform infection counteraction and populace wellbeing the executives.

3. **Auto Industry**

Electric and Independent Vehicles

In the auto business, development is controlling the shift towards manageable and independent transportation. Electric vehicles (EVs) address a noteworthy development that tends to natural worries and lessens reliance on petroleum products. All the while, the improvement of independent vehicles is reshaping the idea of transportation, with developments in man-made reasoning, sensors, and network driving the advancement of self-driving vehicles.

Associated and Savvy Vehicles

The time of associated vehicles, set apart by developments in vehicle-to-everything (V2X) correspondence, guarantees improved security, effectiveness, and client encounters. Brilliant vehicles furnished with cutting edge driver help frameworks (ADAS) and in-vehicle availability rethink the driving experience. These advancements further develop street security as well as prepare for the future mix of brilliant urban areas and savvy transportation frameworks.

Feasible Materials and Assembling

Because of natural worries, development in the car business stretches out to maintainable materials and assembling rehearses. From lightweight materials that upgrade eco-friendliness to eco-accommodating creation processes, the business is effectively investigating inventive answers for decrease its natural impression. This emphasis on manageability lines up with worldwide endeavors to address environmental change and make a more practical future.

4. **Energy Area**

Environmentally friendly power Advances

The energy area is going through a progressive change driven by developments in environmentally friendly power advances. Sun based and wind power developments, combined with progressions in energy capacity frameworks, are reshaping the worldwide energy scene. The push for supportable energy arrangements lines up with the basic to moderate environmental change and decrease dependence on limited petroleum product assets.

Savvy Lattices and Energy The board

Creative arrangements in shrewd lattice innovation and energy the board frameworks are upgrading the age, circulation, and utilization of energy. Brilliant lattices influence computerized correspondence and computerization to upgrade matrix productivity, screen energy utilization continuously, and coordinate environmentally friendly power sources consistently. These developments add to a stronger and supportable energy foundation.

Carbon Catch and Capacity (CCS)

Tending to the test of ozone depleting substance outflows, advancement in the energy area incorporates the improvement of carbon catch and capacity advancements. CCS arrangements intend to catch carbon dioxide outflows from modern cycles and power plants, forestalling their delivery into the environment. This development assumes an essential part in the progress to a low-carbon future and the decarbonization of key enterprises.

5. **Money and Banking**

Fintech Disturbances

The monetary administrations industry is encountering a flood of development, driven by fintech interruptions that influence innovation to upgrade monetary cycles and administrations. Computerized installment arrangements, blockchain applications, and robo-counselors represent how development is changing conventional financial models. These fintech advancements further develop proficiency as well as cultivate monetary incorporation and openness.

Digital currency and Blockchain

The coming of cryptographic money and blockchain innovation has acquainted decentralized and secure arrangements with conventional monetary frameworks. Blockchain's straightforwardness, changelessness, and decentralized nature can possibly reform different monetary cycles, including cross-line exchanges, savvy agreements, and character check. Cryptographic forms of money like Bitcoin address creative ways to deal with computerized monetary standards and decentralized monetary biological systems.

Risk The board and Prescient Investigation

In the domain of money, advancement reaches out to gamble with the board and prescient examination. High level calculations and AI models investigate tremendous datasets to distinguish designs, evaluate dangers, and make information driven forecasts. These advancements upgrade dynamic cycles, further develop misrepresentation recognition, and add to the improvement of stronger monetary frameworks.

6. **Aviation and Avionics**

High level Airplane Plan and Materials

The aviation and flight industry persistently pushes the limits of development in airplane plan and materials. High level composite materials, streamlined advancements, and eco-friendly motor innovations add to the improvement of more maintainable and elite execution airplane. These developments improve eco-friendliness as well as diminish natural effect.

Space Investigation and Commercialization

Development in aviation reaches out past Earth, with space investigation driving mechanical headways and disclosures. Privately owned businesses are entering the space business, cultivating contest and advancement. The improvement of reusable rocket advancements, space the travel industry drives, and the investigation of Mars represent how development is growing the outskirts of room investigation and commercialization.

Air Traffic The executives and Availability

Advancements in air traffic the executives and network are improving the proficiency and security of air travel. Cutting edge aviation authority frameworks, satellite-based route, and in-flight network add to a more interconnected and smoothed out flying biological system. These advancements further develop correspondence, lessen blockage, and streamline air travel courses.

7. **Training Area**

E-Learning Stages and Advanced Schooling

In the training area, development is changing conventional showing models through the appearance of e-learning stages and advanced schooling arrangements. Online courses, virtual homerooms, and intelligent learning devices influence innovation to make instruction more open and adaptable. These developments take special care of assorted learning styles and expand instructive open doors around the world.

Versatile Learning Advances

Developments in versatile learning advances use man-made consciousness and information examination to customize opportunities for growth. These advancements evaluate individual understudy progress, tailor instructive substance to individual requirements, and give continuous criticism. Versatile learning arrangements improve the adequacy of schooling by taking special care of the remarkable qualities and difficulties of every understudy.

Instruction Innovation Environment

The training innovation (EdTech) biological system envelops many developments, from expanded reality for vivid figuring out how to gamification for upgraded commitment. EdTech developments add to a more unique and intuitive learning climate, encouraging inventiveness and decisive reasoning abilities. The combination of innovation in schooling plans understudies for a quickly developing computerized scene.

8. Fabricating Industry

Industry 4.0 and Savvy Assembling

In the assembling business, the fourth modern transformation, frequently alluded to as Industry 4.0, is described by the coordination of advanced innovations into assembling processes. Brilliant assembling includes the utilization of sensors, mechanization, and information examination to make insightful and interconnected creation frameworks. These advancements improve proficiency, decrease squander, and empower ongoing checking of assembling tasks.

3D Printing and Added substance Assembling

Developments in 3D printing and added substance fabricating alter customary creation techniques. These advances empower the making of complex and tweaked items with more noteworthy accuracy and proficiency. From prototyping to the creation of end-use parts, 3D printing advancements smooth out assembling processes and add to the improvement of more maintainable creation strategies.

Advanced mechanics and Computerization

The far and wide reception of advanced mechanics and computerization in assembling represents how development upgrades productivity and accuracy. Advanced mechanics innovations, including cooperative robots (cobots) and independent frameworks, computerize dreary undertakings, further develop creation speed, and upgrade working environment wellbeing. These advancements enable makers to accomplish more elevated levels of efficiency and quality.

C. Teaser on Squid's Jet Propulsion Mechanism

In the profundities of the sea, a strange and enrapturing display unfurls — the squid's stream impetus component. A wonder of nature's designing, this puzzling framework pushes these cephalopods through the water with unrivaled effortlessness and speed. As we leave on an excursion into the complexities of the squid's fly impetus, we disclose an existence where science meets hydrodynamics in a hypnotizing dance of development.

The Artful dance of Fly Impetus

Envision an animal equipped for quick and coordinated developments, easily floating through the submerged domain. This exhibition isn't a result of blades or tails however a shrewd component that tackles the standards of liquid elements — the squid's fly impetus framework. It's an expressive dance of nature where the cephalopod coordinates unpredictable moves involving water as its stage.

Disentangling the Component
Mantle Constriction: The Throbbing Heartbeat

At the core of the squid's fly drive lies the mantle — a strong, cylindrical design that embodies its body. At the point when the squid chooses to leave on an excursion, an ensemble of constrictions swells through the mantle. This throbbing development packs the mantle cavity, removing water in a powerful exploded. The ejection makes a quick and strong stream, driving the squid the other way.

Accuracy Control: Exploring the Profundities

What separates the squid's impetus is its accuracy command over the stream's heading and force. By controlling the direction of its channel and changing the pace of mantle compressions, the squid can explore with momentous deftness. It's a demonstration of the unpredictability of nature's plan — an animal dominating hydrodynamics to turn into a liquid virtuoso in its submerged space.

Biomimicry: Nature's Development Diagram

The squid's fly drive system is in excess of a natural display — it's a development plan ready to be investigated by human resourcefulness. Researchers and architects look into the profundities, propelled by the potential outcomes of mirroring this regular impetus framework. The use of biomimicry, drawing motivation from nature's plans, holds the commitment of upsetting submerged innovation and mechanical technology.

Suggestions for Innovation and Mechanical technology

Submerged Vehicles: Soft Robots of the Profound

Enlivened by the squid's stream impetus, submerged vehicles known as "squid-bots" arise as an innovative wonder. These robots, furnished with adaptable materials and biomimetic drive frameworks, recreate the squid's smooth motions. The soft robots explore submerged scenes with a degree of accuracy and effectiveness beforehand concealed. The marriage of science and innovation in these submerged voyagers flags another time in independent sea-going vehicles.

Aviation Advancement: Taking Off with Squid's Mysteries

Past the sea's profundities, the standards of squid impetus track down reverberation in the unlimited skies. Aeronautics designers dive into the capability of applying squid-motivated plans to airplane impetus frameworks. Envision airplane that can change their drive instruments in view of the standards of squid motion — quick speed increase, exact control, and negligible energy use. The sky turns into a material where nature's insider facts guide the plan of additional effective and versatile flying machines.

Past Innovation: Natural Importance

Squid in Environments: Nature's Difficult exercise

Before we dig further into the mechanical ramifications, appreciating the environmental meaning of squid impetus right at home is pivotal. Squid, as dynamic hunters and prey, assume an imperative part in marine biological systems. Their capacity to quickly explore the sea permits them to take part in complex ways of behaving like hunting, getting away from hunters, and mating. The productivity of squid drive isn't simply a wonder of biomechanical designing; it is a method for surviving finely tuned by development.

Preservation and Moral Contemplations

As we draw motivation from the squid's drive for mechanical development, it becomes basic to think about the moral aspects. Dependable biomimicry includes a guarantee to supportable practices, moral obtaining of materials, and an exhaustive comprehension of the possible ecological effects of mechanical applications. The preservation ramifications of squid biomimicry reach out to both the marine environments that squids possess and the more extensive biological scene.

The Excursion Ahead

As we set out on this excursion into the profundities of the squid's fly impetus system, we wind up at the crossing point of science and innovation. The puzzle of the squid's liquid expressive dance dazzles our creative mind as well as coaxes us to investigate new wildernesses in development. From soft robots exploring sea profundities to airplane taking off through the skies, the squid's insider facts can possibly reshape how we explore and investigate our general surroundings.

Go along with us in disentangling the complexities of this regular impetus framework, where every compression of the mantle reverberations with the heartbeat of advancement. As we plunge into the profundities of revelation, the secrets of the squid's fly drive become a logical wonder as well as a wellspring of motivation for the unlimited potential outcomes that lie at the convergence of nature's resourcefulness and human inventiveness. The excursion has recently started, and the privileged insights of the squid's fly impetus anticipate those prepared to investigate the marvels of biomimicry and mechanical development.

Chapter 1

The Marvel Of Squid Propulsion

The submerged world is a domain of secret and wonder, with its occupants frequently showing surprising transformations for endurance. Among these captivating animals, the squid stands apart for its one of a kind and sensational technique for motion — fly impetus. This mind boggling and effective system, tracked down in different squid species, has enthralled researchers and scientists for a really long time. In this investigation, we will disentangle the wonder of squid impetus, diving into the life systems, physiology, and developmental meaning of this striking variation.

1. **Life structures of Squid:**
   To comprehend squid drive, we should initially look at the life structures of these cephalopods. Squids have a delicate, extended body, known as the mantle, which houses the essential organs. This mantle is the focal point of the impetus cycle. Moreover, squids have strong balances and limbs, adding to their readiness and adaptability in the water.
   The way to squid impetus lies in the mantle, a strong construction liable for producing the power expected for development. Encased inside the mantle is the mantle pit, which assumes a critical part in the drive system. The mantle hole goes about as a chamber for water admission and removal, making the pressure driven force required for quick development.
2. **Stream Impetus Instrument:**
   Squid impetus depends on an interaction known as fly drive, a brilliant transformation that empowers fast and exact development through the water. The interaction starts with the constriction of the mantle muscles, which pack the mantle hole, compelling water out through a siphon-like design known as the channel. This removal of water creates a strong stream that moves the squid the other way.
   The heading of the fly can be constrained by changing the direction of the channel, giving squids extraordinary spryness and mobility. This component permits

squids to explore their submerged surroundings with unmatched speed, making them skilled hunters and tricky prey.

3. **Hydrodynamics of Squid Impetus:**
The effectiveness of squid impetus lies in the hydrodynamics of their developments. As water is strongly removed from the mantle depression, it makes a receptive power that impels the squid forward. This responsive power is tackled by the smoothed out state of the squid's body, limiting opposition and augmenting speed.

The coordination between mantle withdrawal, water removal, and body developments exhibits the accuracy and refinement of squid drive. The hydrodynamic plan of squids has propelled designers and scientists to investigate biomimicry for creating proficient submerged drive frameworks.

4. **Developmental Importance:**
The development of squid drive is a demonstration of the versatile idea of these cephalopods. Through regular choice, squids with more viable fly drive systems enjoyed a cutthroat benefit in catching prey, getting away from hunters, and exploring their environmental elements. Over the long haul, this developmental strain prompted the refinement of the fly impetus framework we see in present day squids.

The capacity to quickly push through the water has likely assumed a critical part in the endurance and outcome of different squid species. The transformative meaning of this variation isn't just clear in the actual design of squids yet in addition in their way of behaving and biological connections.

5. **Near Investigation with Human Impetus Frameworks:**
Contrasting squid impetus with human-made drive frameworks offers experiences into the productivity and development intrinsic in nature. While human impetus strategies frequently depend on mechanical motors and complex hardware, squids have developed a smoothed out, organic component that requires insignificant energy consumption.

Human architects and researchers concentrating on squid drive expect to draw motivation from nature's plan to make more energy-effective and harmless to the ecosystem submerged impetus frameworks. The near investigation opens roads for biomimetic advances that can reform the field of submerged investigation and transportation.

6. **Applications in Biomimicry and Innovation:**
Squid drive fills in as a wellspring of motivation for biomimicry, a discipline that tries to copy nature's answers for complex issues. Scientists and architects are investigating the use of squid-motivated innovation in different fields, going from advanced mechanics to submerged vehicles.

In the field of advanced mechanics, squid-propelled drive frameworks offer the potential for exceptionally nimble and flexibility robots fit for exploring submerged conditions with accuracy. These biomimetic robots could be utilized for logical investigation, natural observing, and even pursuit and salvage missions.

In the domain of submerged vehicles, the proficiency of squid drive has prompted the improvement of bio-roused impetus frameworks for submarines and independent submerged vehicles (AUVs). By emulating the regular developments of squids, these vehicles can accomplish more noteworthy energy proficiency and mobility in submerged conditions.

Aviation design specialists are likewise investigating the use of squid impetus standards in airplane plan. The smoothed out and energy-proficient development of squids through water has suggestions for making more streamlined and eco-friendly airplane.

7. **Challenges in Squid Biomimicry:**

While the likely uses of squid drive in innovation are energizing, there are difficulties that analysts and architects should address. Reproducing the intricacy of an organic framework in a man-made gadget presents inborn troubles. Accomplishing the degree of effectiveness and accuracy saw in squid impetus is a considerable undertaking.

One test lies in the material science part of biomimicry. Creating materials that can endure the powers applied during mantle withdrawal and water removal, while staying adaptable and lightweight, is a basic thought for effective squid-roused innovation.

One more test is the mix of control frameworks that can repeat the refined coordination saw in squid developments. Emulating the brain and strong control systems of squids requires progressed advanced mechanics and computerized reasoning, pushing the limits of current innovative capacities.

8. **Continuous Exploration and Disclosures:**

The field of squid drive is dynamic, with progressing research uncovering new aspects of this amazing transformation. Scientists are investigating the brain processes and solid control components that coordinate the complicated grouping of developments engaged with squid impetus.

Late disclosures remember experiences into the job of explicit muscles for the mantle and the calibrating of water ejection for exact control of development. As innovation progresses, specialists can utilize refined imaging methods and computational demonstrating to dive further into the complexities of squid drive.

9. **Ecological Effect and Moral Contemplations:**

As specialists seek after biomimetic innovations enlivened by squid impetus, moral contemplations and ecological effect should be painstakingly assessed. The turn of events and organization of submerged vehicles and mechanical technology ought to focus on negligible interruption to marine environments.

Moral contemplations stretch out to the possible utilization of squid-enlivened innovation for military or modern purposes. Finding some kind of harmony among advancement and capable utilization of biomimetic innovation is fundamental to keep away from unseen side-effects for marine life and biological systems.

10. **Future Possibilities and Developments:**

The fate of squid-enlivened innovation holds guarantee for earth shattering developments. Proceeded with examination and joint effort between sea life scholars, designers, and technologists are fundamental for beating difficulties and opening the maximum capacity of squid biomimicry.

Developments in material science, advanced mechanics, and man-made brainpower will probably assume an essential part in propelling squid-enlivened innovation. The improvement of commonsense applications, like exceptionally flexibility submerged vehicles and proficient impetus frameworks, is not too far off.

1.1 Overview of Squid Anatomy

Squids, individuals from the mollusk class Cephalopoda, are surprising animals occupying the world's seas. With their complicated life structures and modern variations, squids have fascinated researchers and marine fans the same. This investigation gives a top to bottom outline of squid life systems, digging into their outer and inner designs, and the extraordinary elements that empower these cephalopods to flourish in different marine conditions.

1. **Outside Elements:**

Mantle:

The mantle, a conspicuous element of squid life systems, is a strong cylinder that incorporates the squid's body. Situated dorsally, the mantle encases crucial organs and assumes a vital part in fly impetus, a striking movement system novel to squids.

Balances:

Squids are furnished with different blades, adding to their dexterity and mobility in the water. The essential balances incorporate the three-sided formed dorsal blade, parallel balances at the edges of the mantle, and the caudal blade at the back end. These blades work couple, giving solidness and control during development.

Limbs and Arms:

Squids have two particular kinds of extremities: long, adaptable appendages and more limited, more various arms. Appendages are frequently utilized for catching prey, including specific suckers along their length. Arms, then again, help with controlling and getting food.

Bill and Radula:

The squid's bill is a hard, parrot-like design situated at the focal point of the foundation of the arms. This bill is utilized for getting a handle on and tearing prey. Furthermore, squids have a radula, a toothed strip like design inside the mouth, helping with the breakdown of food before ingestion.

Siphon:

Situated on the ventral side of the mantle, the siphon is a rounded design through which water is removed during plane drive. The siphon's direction permits squids to control the heading of the ousted water, working with exact developments.

2. **Interior Designs:**

Mantle Pit:

The mantle pit is a focal part of squid life structures, lodging basic organs like the gills and the channel. It fills in as the center point for water admission and ejection during breath and impetus.

Gills:

Squids breathe through gills, which remove oxygen from water for metabolic cycles. Gills are housed inside the mantle pit and are furnished with multifaceted designs for proficient gas trade.

Stomach related Framework:

The stomach related arrangement of squids incorporates a throat, stomach, and caecum. Food is first gotten a handle on by the arms and limbs, then, at that point, torn by the bill, and further separated in the stomach. The caecum, a stomach related organ, helps with supplement ingestion.

Circulatory Framework:

Squids have a shut circulatory framework, involving a three-chambered heart that siphons blue, copper-based hemolymph all through the body. Hemolymph assumes a double part in shipping oxygen and supplements while likewise filling in as a pressure driven liquid for the mantle withdrawal during plane impetus.

Sensory system:

Squids have an exceptionally evolved sensory system, including an intricate cerebrum and an organization of ganglia. The mind, situated in the head area, is answerable for handling tactile data and organizing different engine capabilities, adding to the squid's astounding knowledge.

Regenerative Framework:

The regenerative arrangement of squids is specific, with particular sexual dimorphism. Male squids move spermatophores to the female utilizing a changed arm, and females store the sperm until preparation. The eggs are then laid in coagulated cases, guaranteeing security and improvement until bring forth.

3. **Particular Variations:**

Chromatophores:

One of the most unmistakable elements of squid life systems is the presence of chromatophores — shade holding cells inside the skin. Constrained by muscles, these phones permit squids to quickly change tone and examples for correspondence, cover, and flagging.

Statocysts:

Squids use statocysts, specific organs containing little calcareous designs, to keep up with equilibrium and direction in the water. These tactile designs give vital data to the squid's spatial mindfulness.

Ink Sac:

Squids have an ink sac, a cautious variation used to prevent hunters. When compromised, squids remove a haze of ink into the water, making a distraction that permits them to escape from expected dangers.

Photophores:

Certain squid species have photophores, light-emanating organs that guide in bioluminescence. These designs are decisively situated on the body and appendages, filling different needs, including correspondence, drawing in prey, or befuddling hunters.

4. **Developmental Importance:**

The multifaceted highlights of squid life systems have advanced more than huge number of years, driven by the powers of regular choice. The flexibility and adaptability presented by these designs have been fundamental for squids to flourish in assorted marine biological systems.

The improvement of specific extremities, the development of the ink sac as a safeguard component, and the refinement of the fly impetus framework feature the effective variation of squids to their biological specialties. The multifaceted equilibrium of outside and inside structures highlights the developmental excursion that has molded these cephalopods into proficient and exceptionally competent marine life forms.

5. **Environmental Collaborations:**

Squid life systems assumes a critical part in the biological connections inside marine environments. As the two hunters and prey, squids add to the mind boggling food web of the seas. Their capacity to quickly explore through the water, joined with their high level tactile and protective variations, positions them as vital participants in keeping up with the equilibrium of marine environments.

As hunters, squids effectively chase more modest marine organic entities, showing momentous coordination between their arms, limbs, and nose. Alternately, as prey, their quick developments and guarded systems, for example, ink discharge and chromatophore variety changes, assist them with sidestepping hunters going from fish to marine warm blooded animals.

1.2 Exploration of Squid's Unique Jet Propulsion System

The submerged domain is home to a heap of entrancing animals, each outfitted with specific variations for endurance. Among these occupants, squids stand apart for their extraordinary stream impetus framework — a developmental wonder that empowers these cephalopods to explore the seas with unrivaled speed and nimbleness. This investigation dives into the perplexing subtleties of the squid's interesting plane drive framework, unwinding the biomechanics, physiological cycles, and natural meaning of this unprecedented variation.

1. **Developmental Foundations of Stream Drive:**
   The fly impetus framework saw in squids is a result of millions of long periods of developmental refinement. This variation has furnished squids with an upper hand in catching prey, getting away from hunters, and exploring their submerged surroundings with wonderful proficiency.

   The developmental foundations of stream drive can be followed back to the hereditary mollusks from which squids have advanced. As these marine living beings experienced different difficulties in their territories, regular determination leaned toward people with upgraded versatility. After some time, the mantle hole and related muscles went through alterations, coming full circle in the advancement of the refined stream drive framework found in present day squids.

2. **Life structures of Squid's Fly Drive Framework:**
   Mantle Muscles:
   At the core of the fly drive framework lies the strong mantle, a solid construction encompassing the squid's body. The mantle houses the fundamental muscles liable for producing the power expected for drive. Withdrawal of these muscles starts the removal of water from the mantle cavity.

   Mantle Depression:
   The mantle depression fills in as the focal chamber for water admission and removal during plane impetus. This hole is unpredictably associated with the gills, considering effective oxygen trade while additionally working with the removal of water for development.

   Channel or Siphon:
   Situated at the back finish of the mantle, the channel, otherwise called the siphon, is a cylindrical design through which water is removed. The direction of the pipe is basic for controlling the course of the stream, furnishing squids with exact command over their developments.

3. **Biomechanics of Squid Impetus:**
   The biomechanics of squid impetus include a progression of facilitated developments and physiological cycles. The succession starts with the compression of the mantle muscles, bringing about a diminishing in the volume of the mantle pit. This compression ousts water effectively through the channel, making a stream impetus impact that drives the squid the other way.

   The ejection of water is a quick and powerful interaction, producing the receptive power vital for positive headway. The smoothed out state of the squid's body limits obstruction, taking into account effective drive through the water. The whole cycle is a demonstration of the accuracy and refinement of the biomechanics involved.

4. **Job of Water Ejection in Squid Movement:**
   The ejection of water serves numerous capabilities in squid motion. Basically, it impels the squid forward, considering quick escapes from hunters or quick quests for prey. The directional control managed the cost of by the direction of the channel empowers squids to explore with dexterity, making them profoundly adroit trackers and dodgers in their submerged surroundings.
   Moreover, the water removal system assumes a significant part in breath. As water is brought into the mantle depression for removal, it disregards the gills, working with oxygen take-up. This double usefulness of the stream impetus framework features the proficiency and versatility of squids in their amphibian territories.

5. **Hydrodynamic Effectiveness of Squid Drive:**
   Squid drive is portrayed by its hydrodynamic effectiveness, a consequence of the smoothed out plan of the squid's body and the accuracy in the coordination of muscle constrictions. The quick ejection of water makes a receptive power that pushes the squid forward, with insignificant opposition from the encompassing water.
   The smoothed out body shape, joined with the stream drive component, permits squids to accomplish great rates. This hydrodynamic productivity is a basic part of their ruthless and shifty methodologies, empowering them to explore vast waters and complex conditions effortlessly.

6. **Accuracy in Stream Impetus:**
   The accuracy saw in squid impetus is a demonstration of the refined coordination of muscles and the tweaked command over the ejection of water. Squids can tweak the power and heading of the stream by changing the compression of explicit mantle muscles and modifying the direction of the pipe.
   This accuracy is especially critical during hunting or hesitant moves. Squids can roll out quick improvements in heading or reach a sudden come by finely controlling the stream impetus process. Such spryness gives a huge benefit in getting prey or keeping away from hunters in the dynamic and serious submerged climate.

7. **Fly Impetus in Various Squid Species:**
   While the essential standards of fly impetus are reliable across squid species, varieties exist in the particular transformations saw in various genera. For instance:
   Goliath Squids:
   Goliath squids, having a place with the Architeuthidae family, are known for their gigantic size and slippery nature. In spite of their size, goliath squids use fly drive for productive velocity. The biomechanics are increased to oblige the bigger mantle and more noteworthy water dislodging expected for drive.
   Humboldt Squids:
   Humboldt squids, or gigantic squids, are exceptionally forceful hunters tracked down in remote ocean conditions. Their fly drive framework is finely tuned for

quick and strong developments, permitting them to seek after schools of fish with surprising pace and nimbleness.

Cuttlefish:

Cuttlefish, direct relations of squids, likewise utilize a stream drive framework. Notwithstanding, cuttlefish have extra variations, for example, a cuttlebone for lightness control and more perplexing chromatophores for refined disguise capacities.

The variety in squid species features the versatility of the fly drive framework to different biological specialties and social systems.

8. **Vigorous Contemplations in Stream Impetus:**

   While fly impetus gives squids a viable method for velocity, it accompanies enthusiastic expenses. The constriction of mantle muscles and the removal of water require huge metabolic energy. Squids should find some kind of harmony between the advantages of fast development and the energy exhausted in performing plane drive.

   To streamline energy use, squids frequently shift back and forth between times of flying and coasting. Coasting permits them to moderate energy while as yet keeping a consistent speed. This energy-productive system is fundamental for the endurance of squids, particularly during long relocations or expanded hunting pursuits.

9. **Social Transformations and Fly Impetus:**

   The fly impetus framework isn't just a device for movement yet in addition a vital part of different conduct transformations in squids. A few striking viewpoints include:

   Ruthless Pursuits:

   Squids use their stream impetus framework for high velocity quests for prey. By quickly shutting the distance to their objective, squids improve the probability of an effective catch. This ruthless way of behaving is essential for their endurance and food.

   Get away from Reactions:

   When confronted with hunters, squids convey their stream drive framework for fast escapes. The abrupt explosion of speed permits them to outsmart and sidestep possible dangers. The directional control managed the cost of by the channel direction is especially important in these break reactions.

   Romance Showcases:

   Stream drive is likewise utilized in romance shows and mating customs. Male squids might take part in intricate presentations, utilizing their streaming skills to exhibit readiness and ability. This social variation is essential to the conceptive progress of squids.

10. **Uses of Squid Stream Impetus in Innovation:**

    The one of a kind stream impetus arrangement of squids has caught the creative mind of designers and specialists, prompting the investigation of biomimetic applications in innovation. By drawing motivation from the regular world, researchers expect to foster imaginative impetus frameworks with applications in different fields:

Submerged Mechanical technology:

Squid-motivated drive frameworks are being read up for applications in submerged advanced mechanics. The spryness and effectiveness of squid movement give a diagram to planning independent submerged vehicles (AUVs) fit for exploring complex conditions for logical examination, investigation, and natural checking.

Aeronautic design:

The standards of fly impetus saw in squids have suggestions for aeronautic design. Scientists are investigating biomimetic plans for airplane impetus frameworks, drawing motivation from the smoothed out body and effective development of squids through water.

Clinical Gadgets:

The flexibility and accuracy of squid stream impetus have possible applications in the improvement of clinical gadgets. Biomimetic plans roused by the muscle control and liquid elements of squid drive could add to developments in microfluidics and clinical inserts.

Search and Salvage Tasks:

Squid-propelled innovation could be used in the advancement of search and salvage robots for submerged activities. The capacity to explore quickly and exactly through submerged conditions is profitable for finding and helping people in trouble.

11. **Difficulties and Future Bearings:**

While the investigation of squid stream impetus in innovation holds guarantee, there are difficulties to survive. Recreating the intricacy of organic frameworks in counterfeit gadgets presents designing and mechanical obstacles. Challenges include:

Material Science:

Creating materials that can endure the powers applied during mantle withdrawal and water removal, while staying lightweight and adaptable, is a critical test in biomimetic designing.

Control Frameworks:

Imitating the refined brain and solid control components of squids requires progressed advanced mechanics and computerized reasoning. Accomplishing the degree of coordination saw in regular fly impetus is a continuous area of exploration.

Natural Effect:

As squid-roused innovations progress, the potential ecological effect should be painstakingly thought of. The organization of submerged vehicles and mechanical technology ought to focus on insignificant interruption to marine environments.

Interdisciplinary Cooperation:

Effective turn of events and execution of squid-enlivened innovation require inter-disciplinary joint effort between sea life scientists, architects, and technologists. A comprehensive methodology, coordinating natural comprehension with designing mastery, is fundamental for defeating difficulties.

The future bearings in the field of squid-propelled innovation include proceeded with examination into the biomechanics and physiological cycles basic stream impetus. Headways in material science, advanced mechanics, and control frameworks will add to the improvement of useful applications with genuine effect.

1.3 Significance of Squid's Propulsion in Evolution

The development of life on Earth is set apart by a steady battle for endurance, driving creatures to foster one of a kind transformations that upgrade their odds of coming out on top in their separate surroundings. Among the numerous striking transformations found in marine life, the drive system of squids holds specific importance. The development of squid drive is a demonstration of the particular tensions of the submerged world, forming these cephalopods into profoundly effective and deft marine hunters. This investigation dives into the meaning of squid's impetus in development, looking at how this variation has added to their biological achievement and versatility.

1. **Endurance Benefit in Predation:**

   Squid's impetus framework developed fundamentally as an instrument for predation. In the far reaching and dynamic climate of the vast sea, fast and exact development is urgent for both hunting and avoiding hunters. Squids, being dynamic hunters themselves, required a successful method for velocity to effectively catch prey.

   The improvement of stream drive in squids gave a particular benefit in predation. By ousting water through their mantle hole, squids create a strong stream that moves them forward. This fast development empowers them to close the hole with prey quickly, improving the probability of effective catches. The capacity to quickly explore the immensity of the vast sea has been a critical consider the transformative progress of squids as hunters.

2. **Flexibility in Hunting Procedures:**

   The meaning of squid drive turns out to be much more evident while considering the adaptability it gives in hunting procedures. Squids are known for their different taking care of propensities, going after various marine creatures, including fish, scavangers, and, surprisingly, different squids. The flexibility of their impetus framework permits squids to fit their hunting methodologies to the attributes of their prey.

   For example, while seeking after quick swimming fish, squids can release explosions of speed utilizing their stream drive to find and catch their prey. On the other hand, in stealthier hunting situations, for example, following more modest organic entities, squids can use exact and controlled developments to move toward their objectives without cautioning them. This flexibility in hunting procedures features the developmental meaning of squid drive in working with a wide range of ruthless ways of behaving.

3. **Avoidance and Guard Instruments:**
   While squids are impressive hunters, they likewise face steady dangers from bigger marine life forms. The development of their drive framework is similarly indispensable for avoidance and guard. When stood up to by hunters, squids can utilize their fly drive to execute fast and erratic departure moves.

   The capacity to take a different path quickly and speed up away from risk improves their possibilities of endurance. Also, squids use cautious methodologies, for example, ink discharge, chromatophore variety changes, and siphon-arranged flying to frustrate and divert hunters. The combination of these protective instruments with stream drive grandstands the developmental weapons contest among squids and their hunters, molding the intricacy of their step by step processes for surviving.

4. **Energy Productivity in Motion:**
   The transformative meaning of squid drive reaches out past predation and guard — it additionally addresses the crucial requirement for effective velocity. In the boundlessness of the sea, where assets might be scattered or packed in unambiguous areas, energy-effective development is essential for endurance.

   Squids have developed a drive framework that limits energy use while boosting pace and mobility. The smoothed out state of their bodies, combined with the accuracy of fly impetus, permits squids to travel through water with insignificant opposition. This energy-effective method of headway gives a transformative benefit by permitting squids to cover extensive distances looking for prey or reasonable territories.

5. **Transformation to Different Conditions:**
   Squids possess many marine conditions, from waterfront waters to the remote ocean. The versatility of their drive framework plays had a critical impact in their capacity to flourish in different natural surroundings. In shallow seaside regions, squids can explore mind boggling conditions with accuracy, using their fly impetus for quick developments in and around submerged structures.

   In the untamed sea and remote ocean domains, where conditions can be testing and prey might be scant, the effectiveness of squid impetus permits them to investigate and take advantage of different biological specialties. The versatility of their velocity framework has worked with the fruitful colonization of various marine conditions, adding to their boundless conveyance.

6. **Regenerative Achievement and Mating Showcases:**
   The meaning of squid drive isn't restricted to endurance — it likewise stretches out to conceptive achievement. During the mating season, squids use their fly impetus framework as a feature of mind boggling romance showcases. Guys

might take part in amazing streaming successions, displaying their nimbleness and ability to draw in possible mates.

The capacity to execute these presentations is characteristic of the general wellbeing and hereditary wellness of the individual, affecting the mate determination process. The transformative association between stream impetus and regenerative achievement features how this variation has become interlaced with different parts of squid conduct and biology.

7. **Commitments to Cephalopod Advancement:**
Squids have a place with the class Cephalopoda, which incorporates different cephalopods like octopuses and cuttlefish. While each gathering has novel transformations, the drive framework found in squids has likely impacted the development of cephalopods in general. Normal precursors might have shown early types of fly drive, and the refinement of this component in squids embodies the versatile radiation that happened inside cephalopod advancement.

The progress of squids in taking advantage of different environmental specialties and embracing various hunting and protection techniques might have added to the developmental radiation of cephalopods. Collectively, cephalopods have exhibited unrivaled mental capacities, complicated ways of behaving, and a wide cluster of transformations, with stream impetus being a foundation of their natural achievement.

8. **Suggestions for Biomimicry and Innovation:**
Past its natural importance, the impetus arrangement of squids has ignited interest in biomimicry and mechanical advancement. Specialists and scientists seek nature for motivation, trying to duplicate the productivity and accuracy of squid impetus in submerged advances.

The investigation of squid motion has suggestions for the plan of independent submerged vehicles (AUVs) and submerged mechanical technology. Squid-propelled drive frameworks can possibly alter the field, empowering the advancement of profoundly coordinated and energy-effective submerged vehicles equipped for exploring complex conditions.

9. **Preservation and Biological Equilibrium:**

Understanding the developmental meaning of squid impetus additionally has suggestions for preservation and keeping up with biological equilibrium. Squids assume a vital part in marine biological systems as the two hunters and prey, adding to the complicated snare of life in the seas.

Protection endeavors that think about the natural job of squids and their one of a kind transformations, including plane impetus, are fundamental for safeguarding the wellbeing and equilibrium of marine environments. Safeguarding the territories where squids flourish is significant for guaranteeing their proceeded with commitment to the biodiversity and steadiness of the seas.

Chapter 2

Biomimicry And Innovation

Biomimicry, the act of attracting motivation from nature to settle human difficulties, has arisen as a strong power driving development across different fields. By noticing and impersonating the plans, cycles, and frameworks tracked down in the regular world, specialists, architects, and fashioners look for feasible answers for complex issues. This investigation digs into the standards of biomimicry, its verifiable roots, and the groundbreaking effect it has on development, manageability, and the journey for an agreeable conjunction with the planet.

1. **Authentic Underlying foundations of Biomimicry:**
   The idea of biomimicry is certainly not a new peculiarity yet has profound verifiable roots, with early models tracked down in old civic establishments. Native people group noticed and imitated the way of behaving of creatures and plants to foster proficient apparatuses, covers, and rural practices. Be that as it may, the formalization of biomimicry as a logical and configuration discipline picked up speed in the last 50% of the twentieth hundred years.

   Velcro and Biomimicry's Ascent:
   The cutting edge second for biomimicry in present day times can be followed back to the 1940s when Swiss architect George de Mestral saw how burdock seeds stuck to his canine's fur and his own dress. Interested by the regular component, he created Velcro, a snare and-circle securing framework that mirrored the seed's connection. This development denoted a critical achievement, starting interest in the capability of imitating nature's plans for human advantage.

   Janine Benyus and Biomimicry as a Discipline:
   The expression "biomimicry" was advocated by researcher and writer Janine Benyus in her notable book "Biomimicry: Advancement Propelled Commonly," distributed in 1997. Benyus supported for a change in context, encouraging researchers and fashioners to see nature not just as a wellspring of assets but rather as a tutor, offering reliable answers for mind boggling difficulties. This

established the groundwork for biomimicry as a proper discipline, encouraging interdisciplinary joint efforts among scholars, designers, engineers, and materials researchers.

2. **Standards of Biomimicry:**

Biomimicry is directed by a bunch of crucial rules that shape its way to deal with development. These standards underline the significance of imitating nature's methodologies, designs, cycles, and frameworks to make manageable and regenerative arrangements.

Nature as a Model:

The center standard of biomimicry lies in nature as a model. By concentrating on the structures and elements of life forms, biological systems, and normal cycles, biomimics look for experiences that can be converted into creative plans and innovations. Nature's 3.8 billion years of innovative work act as a priceless archive of maintainable arrangements.

Nature as a Guide:

Biomimicry energizes a change in context from survey nature as a distribution center of assets to considering it to be a tutor. By perceiving the insight implanted in the regular world, trailblazers gain motivation for planning arrangements that are successful as well as lined up with the flexibility and productivity saw in biological systems.

Supportable Arrangements:

One of the general objectives of biomimicry is to foster supportable arrangements that imitate the productivity, circularity, and versatility tracked down in regular frameworks. By coordinating standards of regenerative plan, biomimetic advancements expect to limit natural effect, moderate assets, and add to the general soundness of the planet.

Environment Administrations and Capabilities:

Biomimicry reaches out past individual creatures to consider whole biological systems and the administrations they give. Emulating the interconnectedness, variety, and usefulness of environments can prompt advancements that address complex difficulties while advancing flexibility and biodiversity.

3. **Biomimicry in Various Disciplines:**

Biomimicry has tracked down applications across a different exhibit of disciplines, igniting developments in materials science, design, designing, medication, and then some. The cross-fertilization of thoughts among nature and human creativity has brought about extraordinary forward leaps that exhibit the flexibility of biomimicry.

Materials Science:

Nature is an expert of material science, creating structures with surprising strength, adaptability, and lightweight properties. Biomimetic materials, enlivened by substances tracked down in nature, have been created for applications going from advanced plane design to buyer items. Models incorporate bio-roused cements, self-mending materials, and lightweight composites demonstrated after the design of bones.

Engineering and Plan:

Draftsmen and planners draw motivation from the effectiveness and style of regular designs while making reasonable and tough structures. The biomimetic plan standards have prompted developments, for example, building plans that upgrade normal ventilation, emulate termite hills for temperature guideline, and integrate biomorphic designs for energy effectiveness.

Transportation and Aviation:

Biomimicry has affected transportation arrangements by copying the productivity of regular frameworks. For example, the plan of rapid trains has been impacted by the smoothed out state of kingfisher bills, lessening air opposition. In aviation, analysts are investigating the wing plans of birds and bats to improve the productivity and mobility of airplane.

Clinical Developments:

The field of medication has seen noteworthy biomimetic developments, from bio-motivated prosthetics and inserts to sedate conveyance frameworks displayed after normal cycles. The investigation of natural frameworks has propelled progressions in clinical imaging, tissue designing, and medication advancement.

Energy and Asset The executives:

Biomimicry offers answers for reasonable energy age and asset the executives. Developments enlivened by photosynthesis, like fake leaves for sunlight based energy change, show the potential for tackling nature's cycles to meet human energy needs. Also, methodologies got from biological systems, similar to supplement cycling, illuminate practical ways to deal with squander the executives.

4. **Contextual analyses in Biomimicry:**

A few convincing contextual investigations delineate the groundbreaking effect of biomimicry on development across various spaces. These models exhibit how bits of knowledge from nature can prompt pivotal arrangements with the possibility to address squeezing worldwide difficulties.

Biomimicry in Engineering: The Eastgate Center (Termite-motivated Cooling):

The Eastgate Center in Harare, Zimbabwe, planned by draftsman Mick Pearce, draws motivation from termite hills for its cooling framework. Termites build hills with a novel ventilation framework that manages temperature. The Eastgate Center copies this methodology, utilizing uninvolved cooling strategies to lessen energy utilization. The structure's plan has exhibited critical energy reserve funds, displaying the adequacy of biomimicry in engineering advancement.

Biomimicry in Transportation: The Shinkansen (Kingfisher-motivated Slug Train):

The plan of the Shinkansen, Japan's rapid shot train, was affected by the kingfisher bird. Engineers looked to diminish the commotion made when the train left burrows at high rates. By demonstrating the front of the train after the smoothed out state of a kingfisher's mouth, they limited pneumatic stress changes, bringing about calmer and more proficient train travel.

Biomimicry in Materials Science: Geckskin (Gecko-roused Glue):

Geckos are known for their astounding skill to grip to surfaces utilizing a large number of minuscule hairs on their feet. Enlivened by this regular cement instrument, scientists created Geckskin, a reusable and solid glue that copies the gecko's grasping capacities. This development has possible applications in regions like advanced mechanics, clinical gadgets, and shopper items.

Biomimicry in Medication: Velcro and Blood Coagulating (Nature-roused Clinical Glues):

The advancement of clinical glues, like Velcro, drew motivation from nature. Velcro's snare and-circle framework reflects the burdock seed's connection component, while clinical cements for wound conclusion have been roused by the manner in which blood platelets stick to harmed tissue. These biomimetic approaches offer options in contrast to customary stitches and staples, giving effective and less obtrusive clinical arrangements.

5. **Moral Contemplations and Biomimicry:**

While biomimicry holds colossal commitment for practical development, taking into account moral ramifications in its application is critical. The dependable and careful act of biomimicry includes cautious thought of natural effect, regard for biodiversity, and coordinated effort with native networks and neighborhood information.

Preservation of Biodiversity:

Biomimicry depends on the perception and investigation of living life forms. Be that as it may, moral worries emerge when the training possibly adds to the overexploitation of specific species or biological systems. Mindful biomimicry stresses the protection of biodiversity and empowers moral obtaining of organic motivations.

Social Apportionment and Native Information:

Native people group have a long history of noticing and gaining from nature, adding to a rich embroidery of conventional information. Biomimicry experts should be aware of social apportionment and look for conscious joint effort with native networks. Incorporating native information can improve the moral underpinning of biomimicry rehearses.

Natural Effect:

The turn of events and use of biomimetic advancements ought to think about their in general natural effect. While biomimicry means to make practical arrangements, potentially negative results or environmental interruptions might happen. A thorough life-cycle investigation is fundamental to evaluate the ecological impression of biomimetic developments.

6. **The Eventual fate of Biomimicry and Development:**

Biomimicry is ready to assume a significant part in molding the eventual fate of development, manageability, and the mission for a more agreeable connection among humankind and the regular world. As mechanical headways proceed, the accompanying regions feature the possible direction and effect of biomimicry on future advancement:

High level Materials and Nanotechnology:

Biomimicry is supposed to drive leap forwards in cutting edge materials and nanotechnology. Specialists are investigating bio-motivated materials with phenomenal strength, adaptability, and self-mending properties. Nanotechnology, propelled by organic cycles at the sub-atomic level, holds guarantee for making imaginative arrangements in medication, hardware, and materials science.

Roundabout Economy Arrangements:

Biomimicry standards adjust intimately with the idea of a roundabout economy, where assets are used productively, squander is limited, and environments are regarded. Future advancements might zero in on biomimetic methodologies for shut circle frameworks, squander decrease, and economical asset the executives.

Environmental Change Moderation and Variation:

Biomimicry offers likely answers for tending to the difficulties of environmental change. Developments motivated by regular cycles, for example, carbon sequestration methodologies saw in plants, may add to environmental change moderation endeavors. Also, biomimetic ways to deal with versatile foundation and metropolitan arranging can help variation to changing environment conditions.

Interdisciplinary Cooperation:

The future of biomimicry lies in expanded interdisciplinary cooperation. As researchers, architects, creators, and scholars cooperate, the potential for groundbreaking advancements develops. Cross-disciplinary associations can prompt more comprehensive arrangements that consider both the specialized possibility and environmental effect of biomimetic plans.

Training and Mindfulness:

Training and mindfulness drives are critical for the proceeded with development of biomimicry. Incorporating biomimicry standards into instructive educational plans and cultivating mindfulness among people in the future can move a mentality shift toward feasible and nature-motivated arrangements.

Strategy and Guideline:

As biomimicry turns out to be more essential to development, there is a requirement for strategies and guidelines that help moral and economical practices. States and organizations might assume a part in laying out rules for the moral utilization of biomimicry, addressing concerns connected with biodiversity, social apportionment, and ecological effect.

Worldwide Coordinated effort for Maintainable Turn of events:

Biomimicry can possibly add to worldwide manageable advancement objectives. Cooperative endeavors on a worldwide scale can outfit the assorted mastery and biodiversity tracked down across various areas. Biomimicry can be an impetus for shared answers for address worldwide difficulties, including clean energy, water shortage, and biodiversity protection.

2.1 Introduction to Biomimicry

Biomimicry, a term got from the Greek words "profiles," meaning life, and "mimesis," importance to impersonate, addresses a progressive way to deal with development propelled by the regular world. It includes noticing, understanding, and imitating the plans, cycles, and techniques tracked down in biological systems and living beings to tackle human difficulties. Basically, biomimicry takes advantage of the abundance of information that has advanced north of billions of years in the unpredictable embroidered artwork of life on The planet, offering economical and regenerative answers for complex issues.

1. **Groundworks of Biomimicry: Gaining from Nature's Virtuoso**

   Nature as a Tutor:

   At the core of biomimicry lies the significant acknowledgment that nature isn't simply an asset to be taken advantage of yet a tutor whose arrangements have endured for an extremely long period. Rather than survey the regular world as a stockroom of unrefined components, biomimicry welcomes us to embrace another point of view — one that sees nature as a tutor offering dependable techniques for proficiency, strength, and flexibility.

   Verifiable Roots:

   While the expression "biomimicry" acquired unmistakable quality in the late twentieth 100 years, the training has profound verifiable roots. Native people group, over the entire course of time, have sought nature for motivation in creating apparatuses, building asylums, and creating reasonable rural practices. The formalization of biomimicry as a logical discipline and plan reasoning, notwithstanding, picked up speed in ongoing many years.

   One of the early forward leaps that caught the world's consideration was the creation of Velcro during the 1940s. Swiss architect George de Mestral drew motivation from the manner in which burdock seeds stuck to his attire and his canine's fur. This development denoted the start of present day biomimicry and laid the basis for a groundbreaking way to deal with critical thinking.

   Janine Benyus and Biomimicry's Renaissance:

   The advanced renaissance of biomimicry owes a lot to scientist and creator Janine Benyus. In her fundamental work, "Biomimicry: Development Propelled Essentially," distributed in 1997, Benyus spread out the basic standards and methods of reasoning of biomimicry. Her work turned into an impetus for a change in context, encouraging researchers, specialists, and creators to shift focus over to nature for motivation as well as an aide for making an additional supportable and amicable future.

2. **Standards of Biomimicry: Copying Nature's Insight**
Nature as Model:
Biomimicry starts with the affirmation that nature is a tremendous store of cunning arrangements. By concentrating on the structures, designs, and cycles of organic entities, biomimics gain bits of knowledge that can be applied to address human difficulties. From the streamlined features of bird wings to oneself mending properties of specific plants, nature gives a different cluster of models for development.

Nature as Measure:
Nature's effectiveness turns into a benchmark for biomimicry. The flexibility, asset productivity, and manageability saw in regular frameworks set a norm for human-planned arrangements. Biomimicry supports the improvement of advancements and cycles that action up to the tastefulness and viability of the normal world.

Reasonable Arrangements:
The all-encompassing objective of biomimicry is to make feasible arrangements that address prompt difficulties as well as contribute decidedly to the general soundness of the planet. Embracing the round and regenerative standards tracked down in biological systems, biomimetic plans endeavor to limit ecological effect, preserve assets, and backing the prosperity of the two individuals and the planet.

Environment Administrations and Capabilities:
Biomimicry expands its look past individual creatures to think about whole biological systems. By getting it and imitating the administrations and capabilities given by environments, biomimicry intends to make developments that add to the strength and variety of life. Biological system enlivened arrangements frequently have a more comprehensive and incorporated way to deal with critical thinking.

3. **Utilizations of Biomimicry: A Cross-Disciplinary Methodology**
Materials Science:
Nature is an expert skilled worker with regards to materials. Biomimicry in materials science includes imitating the properties of normal substances, prompting advancements, for example, bio-enlivened cements, self-recuperating materials, and lightweight composites. The strength of arachnid silk and the flexibility of shells have enlivened the advancement of strong and feasible materials.

Engineering and Plan:
Biomimicry in engineering and configuration draws motivation from the productivity and feel of normal designs. Structures planned with biomimicry standards might advance regular ventilation, manage temperature like termite hills, or consolidate biomorphic designs for energy proficiency. These plans lessen natural effect as well as make spaces that orchestrate with the encompassing environments.

Transportation and Aviation:

The transportation area has embraced biomimicry to upgrade productivity and diminish natural effect. The plan of fast trains, similar to Japan's Shinkansen, took motivation from the smoothed out state of kingfisher noses to limit air opposition and commotion. In aviation, analysts investigate bird and bat wing plans for more effective and flexibility airplane.

Clinical Advancements:

Biomimicry has prompted noteworthy developments in medication. Prosthetics and inserts enlivened by regular designs give more utilitarian and biocompatible arrangements. Clinical glues, demonstrated after the instruments of blood thickening, offer options in contrast to customary stitches. The investigation of natural frameworks illuminates progressions in clinical imaging, drug conveyance, and tissue designing.

Energy and Asset The executives:

Biomimicry standards are applied to address difficulties in energy age and asset the executives. Bio-enlivened advancements, like fake leaves for sun oriented energy change, draw from photosynthesis. Systems got from environments, similar to supplement cycling, move supportable ways to deal with squander the executives and preservation.

4. **Moral Contemplations and the Fate of Biomimicry:**

Protection of Biodiversity:

As biomimicry depends on the perception and investigation of living organic entities, moral worries emerge in regards to likely effects on biodiversity. Mindful biomimicry stresses the preservation of species and biological systems, guaranteeing that the training contributes decidedly to worldwide endeavors to safeguard and support biodiversity.

Social Assignment and Native Information:

Native people group have a rich history of noticing and gaining from nature. The moral act of biomimicry includes regarding and working together with native information. Mindful biomimicry tries to keep away from social assignment and recognizes the commitments of native networks to the field.

Natural Effect:

The turn of events and use of biomimetic innovations ought to think about their by and large ecological effect. While biomimicry holds back nothing, results or biological interruptions might happen. A far reaching life-cycle examination is fundamental to survey the natural impression of biomimetic developments.

Worldwide Coordinated effort for Reasonable Turn of events:

Biomimicry can possibly contribute essentially to worldwide reasonable improvement objectives. Worldwide joint effort can outfit assorted skill and biodiversity from various locales. Biomimicry can be an impetus for shared answers for address worldwide difficulties, including environmental change, clean energy, and biodiversity preservation.

2.2 Examples of Successful Biomimicry in Technology

Biomimicry, the act of attracting motivation from nature to settle human difficulties, has prompted astounding leap forwards in different mechanical fields. By imitating the productivity, flexibility, and versatility viewed as in the normal world, trend-setters have made arrangements that address current difficulties as well as add to an additional supportable and agreeable future.

Velcro and Burdock Seeds:

One of the earliest and most notorious instances of biomimicry is Velcro, roused by the manner in which burdock seeds stick to attire and creature fur. Swiss specialist George de Mestral noticed the regular snare and-circle system of the seeds and duplicated it in Velcro. This straightforward yet compelling plan has tracked down broad use in affixing applications, from shoes to space missions.

Shinkansen Shot Train and Kingfisher Snout:

The fast Shinkansen shot train in Japan took motivation from the kingfisher bird's bill to lessen commotion and increment proficiency. By impersonating the smoothed out state of the kingfisher's snout, engineers overhauled the front of the train to limit air obstruction and choppiness while entering and leaving burrows. This biomimetic plan further developed execution as well as upgraded the general maintainability of fast rail travel.

Lotus-Impact Covering for Self-Cleaning Surfaces:

The lotus plant's capacity to repulse water and stay clean in sloppy conditions enlivened the advancement of self-cleaning surfaces. The lotus-impact covering mirrors the minuscule construction of lotus leaves, making a surface that repulses water and forestalls the grip of soil and foreign substances. This biomimetic innovation has been applied to compositional surfaces, vehicle coatings, and even attire, lessening the requirement for water and compound cleaning.

Biomimetic Materials and Bug Silk:

Insect silk is eminent for its solidarity, adaptability, and lightweight properties. Researchers have looked to repeat these properties in biomimetic materials with applications in medication, materials, and development. By understanding the sub-atomic design of arachnid silk, analysts have made engineered variants that display comparable solidarity to-weight proportions, preparing for creative materials in different businesses.

Bionic Blade for Submerged Investigation:

Propelled by the drive components of fish, especially the undulating movement of a fish's tail blade, engineers fostered a bionic balance for submerged investigation. The bionic blade emulates the regular development of fish balances and is utilized in submerged drones and independent vehicles. This biomimetic configuration upgrades mobility and proficiency in submerged conditions, considering more viable investigation and observing.

Gecko-Propelled Cements:

Geckos are known for their wonderful capacity to climb vertical surfaces and stick to roofs. Specialists have created gecko-roused cements that impersonate the minute design of gecko footpads. These cements have been utilized in mechanical technology, clinical gadgets, and even customer items, giving a reusable and proficient option in contrast to customary glues.

Biomimicry in Wind Turbine Cutting edges:

The plan of wind turbine cutting edges has been affected by the design of humpback whale flippers. The tubercles (knocks) on the main edge of humpback whale flippers enlivened the production of turbine cutting edges with comparative knocks. This biomimetic configuration works on streamlined execution, decreases clamor, and expands the proficiency of wind turbines, adding to the headway of supportable energy arrangements.

These models feature the different uses of biomimicry in innovation, representing how nature's plans and procedures can motivate imaginative arrangements across different businesses. As the field of biomimicry keeps on developing, analysts and architects are probably going to find significantly more chances to draw from the well of nature's virtuoso for manageable and effective innovative headways.

2.3 Potential Applications of Squid Propulsion in Human Technology

The astounding impetus arrangement of squids, which depends on fly drive for fast and effective development through water, has caught the consideration of researchers and designers looking for motivation for imaginative innovations. Squids, especially those having a place with the cephalopod class, have developed a modern component for fly impetus that permits them to explore the untamed sea with deftness and speed. Investigating the expected utilizations of squid impetus in human innovation uncovers energizing prospects across different fields.

Submerged Advanced mechanics and Independent Vehicles:

The transformation of squid impetus in submerged advanced mechanics and independent vehicles holds extraordinary commitment for improving their mobility and effectiveness. Squids can quickly take a different path and speed by removing water through their mantle depression, a capacity that can be reproduced in submerged vehicles. Emulating squid impetus in these advances could bring about exceptionally spry and flexible vehicles equipped for exploring complex submerged conditions effortlessly.

Submarine Plan and Route:

Squid-roused impetus frameworks could alter the plan and route of submarines. Conventional propeller-driven submarines frequently face difficulties concerning mobility and covertness. By consolidating squid-like stream impetus, submarines could accomplish more exact developments and decreased clamor levels, considering stealthier and more proficient submerged tasks.

Search and Salvage Activities:

Squid-propelled impetus could assume a critical part in search and salvage missions, particularly in testing oceanic conditions. Independent submerged vehicles outfitted with squid-propelled impetus frameworks could quickly explore through trash, submerged structures, and differing flows to arrive at far off areas. This application holds critical potential for working on the speed and adequacy of submerged search and salvage activities.

Marine Investigation and Natural Observing:

Squids occupy different marine conditions, from shallow waterfront waters to the remote ocean. Squid drive innovation could be tackled for marine investigation and natural observing. Independent submerged vehicles furnished with squid-roused impetus frameworks could productively review and gather information in naturally delicate regions, adding to how we might interpret marine biological systems and biodiversity.

Military Applications:

Squid-roused impetus frameworks might track down applications in military advances, especially in submerged observation and reconnaissance. The capacity to move quickly and quietly through water is of vital significance in specific military activities. Squid-roused impetus could be coordinated into submerged robots or vehicles for clandestine missions, giving a strategic benefit in marine conditions.

Hydroponics and Fisheries:

The hydroponics business could profit from squid-enlivened impetus for proficient checking and upkeep of submerged framework, for example, fish ranches. Independent submerged vehicles displayed after squid headway could explore through fish pens and submerged structures, adding to further developed administration and maintainability rehearses in hydroponics.

Advancements in Water Sports and Diversion:

Squid drive innovation may likewise move developments in water sports and sporting exercises. Individual watercraft, like stream skis or submerged bikes, could be planned with squid-like drive frameworks to improve speed, mobility, and by and large client experience. This application could open additional opportunities for water lovers and travelers.

Ecological Cleanup and Remediation:

Squid-enlivened drive frameworks could be applied to upgrade natural cleanup endeavors in waterways. Independent submerged vehicles furnished with this innovation could effectively explore dirtied regions, gathering trash and observing water quality. The flexibility of squid-motivated impetus would make these vehicles compelling apparatuses for ecological remediation.

Motivation for Biomimicry in Designing:

Past unambiguous applications, the investigation of squid drive fills in as a wellspring of motivation for biomimicry in designing. Specialists and analysts can draw bits of knowledge from the many-sided components of squid headway to plan more productive and manageable impetus frameworks across different advancements, adding to progressions in liquid elements and submerged designing.

Chapter 3

The Science Behind Squid Propulsion

Squids, individuals from the cephalopod class, have advanced an unprecedented component for quick and productive submerged development known as fly drive. This novel technique permits squids to explore the sea with exceptional nimbleness, empowering them to catch prey, get away from hunters, and navigate huge spans of water. The science behind squid impetus includes a perplexing interchange of life systems, biomechanics, and liquid elements. Understanding the complexities of this normal impetus framework discloses the miracles of cephalopod velocity as well as holds possible ramifications for biomimicry and mechanical advancement.

1. **Life structures of Squid Drive:**
1. **Mantle Hole and Siphon:**
   Fundamental to squid drive is the mantle, a strong organ lodging the gills and other crucial designs. The mantle hole is a chamber inside the mantle that fills in as a repository for water. The squid's siphon, a cylindrical construction, is associated with the mantle cavity and assumes a vital part in the removal of water.
2. **Strong Compressions:**

Fly drive in squids depends on quick and strong solid constrictions of the mantle. At the point when the roundabout muscles of the mantle contract, the volume of the mantle pit diminishes, compelling water out through the siphon. This ejection of water makes a propulsive power that impels the squid forward.
II. **Biomechanics of Squid Stream Impetus:**

1. **Standards of Squid Velocity:**
   The biomechanics of squid stream drive are administered by crucial standards of liquid elements and Newton's third law of movement. As the squid removes water through its siphon, the traditionalist power pushes the squid the other

way. This activity response system is fundamental to the effectiveness of stream drive in squids.

2. Movable Spout Impact:

Squids display an exceptional capacity to control the course and power of their stream impetus. The siphon goes about as a movable spout, permitting squids to coordinate the ousted water every which way. By adjusting the direction of the siphon, squids can accomplish exact and quick shifts in their swimming course, empowering them to explore complex submerged conditions.

III. Liquid Elements of Squid Fly Drive:

1. Water Removal and Responsive Push:

The removal of water through the siphon produces a receptive push that impels the squid forward. This cycle includes the removal of a high-speed stream of water, making a power the other way as directed by Newton's third regulation. The effectiveness of this impetus framework lies in the fast and facilitated solid constrictions that oust water powerfully.

2. Hydrodynamic Productivity:

Squid drive is described by its hydrodynamic effectiveness, permitting squids to move quickly through water with negligible obstruction. The smoothed out state of the squid's body and the capacity to withdraw their blades add to decreased drag, empowering them to arrive at noteworthy paces. The mix of solid power, flexible spout control, and smoothed out morphology represents the hydrodynamic greatness of squid impetus.

IV. Energetics of Squid Fly Impetus:

1. Metabolic Requests:

The energetics of squid fly impetus include contemplations of the metabolic requests related with quick and strong solid compressions. Squids are known to be profoundly dynamic hunters, and the energy expected for supported stream impetus is huge. The proficiency of their headway is essential for adjusting the energy consumption related with hunting, getting away from hunters, and participating in different ways of behaving.

2. Lightness and Profundity Control:

Squids likewise use their stream impetus framework for lightness and profundity control. By changing the power and length of mantle withdrawals, squids can climb or slide in the water segment. This lightness control is fundamental for enhancing their situation in the water, whether hunting in the profundities or ascending to the surface.

V. Transformations for Fly Drive:

1. **Solid Design:**
   The mantle muscle of squids is very much adjusted for the quick compressions expected for stream impetus. The roundabout muscles of the mantle are profoundly evolved and fit for creating strong powers. The effectiveness of these compressions is fundamental for the powerful ejection of water and the age of responsive push.

2. **Siphon Morphology:**
   The guide of squids shows specific morphology to work with fly drive. An adaptable and extended rounded structure takes into consideration directional control of the ousted water. The capacity to change the direction and state of the siphon adds to the accuracy and spryness of squid movement.

3. **Balances and Mantle Channels:**

The balances of squids, related to the mantle channels, assume a part in coordinating water stream and improving drive. Balances can be withdrawn during strong mantle withdrawals, decreasing drag and expanding the productivity of stream impetus. The coordination among blades and mantle constrictions adds to the generally speaking hydrodynamic presentation of squids.

VI. Social Parts of Squid Drive:

1. **Predation and Hunting:**
   Squid drive is a significant part of their predation procedure. Quick and exact developments worked with by fly drive permit squids to really seek after and catch prey. The capacity to head in a different path quickly is worthwhile while chasing after lithe prey, and the component of shock managed the cost of by fast impetus upgrades hunting achievement.

2. **Get away from Reactions:**

Stream impetus is an essential system for get away from reactions in squids when confronted with likely dangers or hunters. The fast removal of water permits squids to execute sly moves, rapidly changing their situation and evading followers. This guarded conduct features the versatile meaning of stream impetus in upgrading endurance.

VII. Biomimicry and Mechanical Development:

1. **Submerged Mechanical technology:**
   The science behind squid drive has propelled analysts in the field of submerged advanced mechanics. Biomimetic submerged vehicles, intended to imitate the standards of squid velocity, can possibly improve the readiness and productivity

of independent submerged frameworks. These vehicles could be conveyed for different applications, including investigation, observation, and natural checking.

2. **Impetus Frameworks:**

The comprehension of the biomechanics and liquid elements of squid stream drive offers experiences for the improvement of more proficient impetus frameworks in human innovation. Engineers looking to work on submerged vehicles, submarines, and other marine advances can draw motivation from the customizable spout impact and smoothed out morphology saw in squids.

3. **Coordinated Route:**

Squid-propelled drive frameworks could find applications in advancements requiring light-footed route in liquid conditions. From submerged robots to independent vehicles, the standards of squid headway offer a plan for accomplishing quick and exact developments. This can be especially applicable in situations like pursuit and salvage activities or natural investigation.

4. **Lightness Control:**

The lightness control showed by squids through their fly impetus framework has suggestions for the advancement of submerged innovations that require exact profundity control. Biomimetic approaches roused by squid lightness control could add to headways in subs, remotely worked vehicles (ROVs), and other submerged vehicles.

VIII. Difficulties and Future Headings:

1. **Fiery Proficiency:**

While squid impetus is exceptionally viable, the fiery requests related with quick mantle compressions present difficulties. Scientists investigating biomimetic applications should address the harmony among effectiveness and energy use, especially in situations where supported and drawn out impetus is required.

2. **Materials and Mimicry:**

The improvement of materials that recreate the adaptability and usefulness of the squid's mantle and siphon is a vital thought for biomimetic applications. Progresses in materials science will assume a urgent part in making engineered structures equipped for copying the biomechanical properties of squid impetus.

3. **Interdisciplinary Coordinated effort:**

The investigation of squid impetus requires interdisciplinary coordinated effort between scholars, biomechanics specialists, liquid elements analysts, and designers. Future examination headings ought to focus on cooperative endeavors to develop how we might interpret squid velocity and make an interpretation of these experiences into reasonable applications.

3.1 Detailed Explanation of Squid's Mantle Contraction

The mantle compression of squids is a biomechanical wonder that underlies their extraordinary strategy for stream impetus, empowering quick and productive submerged velocity. This complicated and composed solid activity assumes a focal part in the squid's capacity to explore its sea-going climate, whether for hunting prey, getting away from hunters, or controlling lightness. Understanding the definite mechanics of squid mantle compression gives experiences into the complexities of cephalopod velocity and offers motivation for biomimetic applications in submerged innovation.

1. **Life systems of the Squid Mantle:**
1. **Mantle Construction:**
   The mantle is a solid organ found posteriorly in the squid's body, lodging fundamental inward designs like the gills. It is encircled by a defensive sheath of tissue and is liable for different capabilities, including breath, fly impetus, and lightness control.
2. **Roundabout and Outspread Muscles:**

The mantle is made out of both roundabout and spiral muscles. Round muscles, otherwise called cross over muscles, run in rings around the perimeter of the mantle. Outspread muscles expand radially from the focal point of the mantle towards its external edges. The coordination of these muscle bunches is fundamental for the mind boggling mantle compression associated with stream impetus.

II. Commencement of Mantle Withdrawal:

1. **Apprehensive Control:**
   The commencement of mantle withdrawal is heavily influenced by the squid's sensory system. Neurons in the ganglia, a piece of the cephalopod's decentralized sensory system, convey messages to the muscles of the mantle, setting off the withdrawal grouping. The decentralized idea of the sensory system takes into consideration fast and restricted reactions, empowering exact command over the mantle constriction process.
2. **Pacemaker Cells:**

Pacemaker cells inside the mantle assume a critical part in setting the beat of mantle constrictions. These specific cells create electrical motivations that spread through the mantle muscles, planning the timing and grouping of withdrawals. The cadenced movement of pacemaker cells guarantees the normal and successive withdrawal of round and outspread muscles, working with the ejection of water.

III. Arrangement of Squid Mantle Withdrawal:

1. **Round Muscle Compression:**
   The compression arrangement starts with the roundabout muscles. As the

round muscles contract, they diminish the volume of the mantle hole. This decrease in volume prompts an expansion in tension inside the mantle cavity, establishing a controlled climate for the removal of water. The roundabout muscles assume an essential part in starting and keeping up with the strong removal of water during plane impetus.

2. **Outspread Muscle Withdrawal:**
Following the withdrawal of round muscles, the outspread muscles become an integral factor. Spiral muscles run opposite to the roundabout muscles and stretch out from the focal point of the mantle to its external edges. At the point when these spiral muscles contract, they further lessen the volume of the mantle cavity, ousting water all the more strongly through the siphon. The coordination among round and outspread muscle compressions improves the effectiveness of fly drive.

3. **Siphon Elements:**

The siphon, a rounded construction associated with the mantle hole, goes about as the leave point for the removed water. The directional control of the siphon is significant for guiding and moving during plane impetus. The compression of round and outspread muscles impacts the shape and direction of the siphon, permitting squids to change the bearing of water removal.

IV. Biomechanics of Squid Mantle Withdrawal:

1. **Newton's Third Regulation:**
The biomechanics of squid mantle withdrawal comply with Newton's third law of movement, which expresses that for each activity, there is an equivalent and inverse response. With regards to squid headway, the activity includes the intense ejection of water through the siphon, and the response is the propulsive power that drives the squid forward. The fast and composed withdrawal of mantle muscles guarantees the age of adequate responsive push for successful drive.

2. **Flexible Spout Impact:**
The guide of squids goes about as a flexible spout, affecting the course and power of water ejection. By controlling the shape and direction of the siphon, squids can accomplish exact shifts in their swimming course. The biomechanics of the customizable spout impact add to the deftness and flexibility of squid movement, permitting them to explore through complex submerged conditions.

3. **Hydrodynamic Productivity:**

Squid mantle compression is described by hydrodynamic effectiveness, limiting drag and streamlining the propulsive power produced. The smoothed out state of the squid's body, related to the retractable blades, adds to diminished obstruction as the squid travels through water. The biomechanics of mantle constriction, in a joint effort with the general morphology of the squid, epitomize the development of a productive and hydrodynamically smoothed out impetus framework.

V. Energetics of Mantle Compression:

1. **Metabolic Requests:**
   The energetics of mantle constriction include the metabolic requests related with the fast and powerful strong movement. Squids are profoundly dynamic hunters, and the energy use expected for supported fly impetus is critical. The effectiveness of mantle constriction becomes pivotal for adjusting the lively expenses related with hunting, getting away from hunters, and different ways of behaving.

2. **Lightness Control:**

Mantle constriction isn't just engaged with stream drive yet in addition assumes a part in lightness control. By changing the power and length of mantle compressions, squids can direct their situation in the water segment. This lightness control is an extra part of the energetics of mantle compression, as squids streamline their situation for different exercises, like hunting or staying away from hunters.

VI. Variations for Effective Stream Impetus:

1. **Solid Engineering:**
   The proficiency of mantle compression is worked with by the particular solid design of squids. Round muscles, with their ring-like plan, produce the underlying power for diminishing mantle hole volume. Spiral muscles, stretching out from the middle to the external edges, add to the further decrease in volume, improving the power of water ejection. The planned activity of these muscles mirrors the transformation of mantle constriction for productive stream impetus.

2. **Morphology of the Siphon:**
   The morphology of the siphon is adjusted for proficient water removal. The rounded construction considers the fast and coordinated arrival of water, while its adaptability adds to the flexible spout impact. The siphon's dynamic shape changes, affected by the compression of mantle muscles, empower squids to control the course and power of water removal with accuracy.

3. **Balances and Mantle Pipes:**

The cooperation among blades and mantle withdrawal upgrades the productivity of fly impetus. Balances, when withdrawn during strong mantle withdrawals, lessen drag and smooth out the squid's body. Mantle pipes, structures related with the mantle, help with coordinating water stream. The organized developments of blades and mantle pipes add to the in general hydrodynamic greatness of squid headway.

VII. Social Parts of Mantle Compression:

1. **Hunting and Prey Catch:**
   Mantle compression is a critical part of the hunting procedure utilized by squids. While hunting prey, squids use mantle withdrawal to push themselves toward their objective quickly. The powerful ejection of water makes an explosion of speed, permitting squids to close the distance to their prey with accuracy. The capacity to control the bearing of water ejection upgrades their hunting achievement.
2. **Get away from Reactions:**

Mantle constriction is a necessary piece of the squid's break reactions when confronted with expected dangers or hunters. The fast and strong removal of water empowers squids to execute equivocal moves, changing their position rapidly and evading followers. This cautious conduct features the flexibility and adaptability of mantle compression in upgrading the endurance chances of squids.

VIII. Biomimicry and Mechanical Development:

1. **Biomimetic Submerged Vehicles:**
   The nitty gritty clarification of squid mantle constriction fills in as motivation for biomimetic applications in submerged innovation. Specialists and analysts keen on working on the proficiency of submerged vehicles, submarines, and independent submerged frameworks can draw experiences from the biomechanics of mantle constriction. Biomimetic submerged vehicles that repeat the movable spout impact and hydrodynamic proficiency of squids can possibly improve readiness and mobility in amphibian conditions.
2. **Drive Frameworks:**
   The comprehension of the biomechanics and liquid elements of squid mantle compression offers significant data for the improvement of more effective drive frameworks in human innovation. Architects can investigate the standards of roundabout and spiral muscle coordination, the customizable spout impact, and smoothed out morphology to plan impetus frameworks that copy the proficiency of cephalopod headway.
3. **Submerged Advanced mechanics:**

Biomimetic approaches enlivened by squid mantle compression have suggestions for the field of submerged advanced mechanics. Independent submerged vehicles intended to imitate the cadenced and strong mantle constrictions of squids could accomplish upgraded nimbleness and accuracy in submerged investigation and observation. The biomimetic mix of movable spouts could additionally add to the adaptability of these mechanical frameworks.

IX. Difficulties and Future Headings:

1. **Copying Cadenced Constrictions:**
Reproducing the cadenced and composed compressions of roundabout and spiral muscles represents a test in biomimetic applications. Accomplishing a consistent mix of these muscle activities in counterfeit frameworks requires a nitty gritty comprehension of the brain control and biomechanics engaged with squid mantle compression.

2. **Materials and Adaptability:**
Creating materials that imitate the adaptability and usefulness of the squid's mantle and siphon is a basic thought for biomimetic plans. Progresses in materials science, including the making of engineered structures that can flex and agreement with comparable effectiveness, are fundamental for fruitful biomimicry.

3. **Interdisciplinary Joint effort:**

The complete comprehension of squid mantle compression requires interdisciplinary cooperation between scientists, biomechanics specialists, neuroscientists, and architects. Future examination bearings ought to focus on cooperative endeavors to unwind the intricacies of squid motion and make an interpretation of these experiences into commonsense applications.

3.2 Role of Water Ejection in Generating Thrust

Water launch is the key component behind the age of pushed in squid fly impetus, an exceptional transformation that permits these cephalopods to explore through water with readiness and speed. Understanding the complexities of how water ejection adds to push gives experiences into the biomechanics of squid velocity and offers motivation for biomimetic applications in submerged innovation.

1. **Standards of Fly Drive:**
1. **Newton's Third Regulation:**
The age of pushed in squid fly drive complies with Newton's third law of movement, which expresses that for each activity, there is an equivalent and inverse response. With regards to squid velocity, the activity includes the powerful ejection of water through the siphon, and the response is the propulsive power that drives the squid forward. The standards of Newton's third regulation administer the elements of pushed age during water discharge.

2. **Traditionalist Push:**

As squids contract their mantle muscles, the volume of the mantle hole diminishes, making expanded strain inside. This expanded tension powers water out through the guide in a strong fly. The removal of water in one bearing makes a traditionalist push the other way, impelling the squid forward. The productivity of this activity response component is essential for the quick and controlled developments of squids in their submerged climate.

II. Water Launch Interaction:

1. **Roundabout Muscle Withdrawal:**
   The water discharge process starts with the compression of roundabout muscles in the mantle. As these muscles contract, they decrease the volume of the mantle depression. This decrease in volume prompts an expansion in tension inside the cavity, establishing a controlled climate for the removal of water. The round muscle constriction is the underlying move toward the arrangement of occasions that come full circle in water launch.

2. **Spiral Muscle Compression:**
   Following the constriction of roundabout muscles, outspread muscles become possibly the most important factor. Spiral muscles expand radially from the focal point of the mantle towards its external edges. At the point when these muscles contract, they further decrease the volume of the mantle cavity, removing water all the more strongly through the siphon. The coordination among roundabout and spiral muscle compressions upgrades the productivity of water discharge and, thus, push age.

3. **Siphon Elements:**

The siphon, a rounded design associated with the mantle pit, goes about as the leave point for the ousted water. The elements of the siphon assume a pivotal part in coordinating the water stream and impacting the subsequent push. Squids can change the direction and state of the siphon, taking into account exact command over the bearing and power of water removal. The flexibility of the siphon adds to the readiness and adaptability of squid velocity.

III. Biomechanics of Water Launch:

1. **Movable Spout Impact:**
   The guide of squids capabilities as a movable spout, affecting the heading and power of water ejection. By changing the shape and direction of the siphon, squids can accomplish exact shifts in their swimming course. The biomechanics of the movable spout impact add to the spryness and flexibility of squid movement, permitting them to explore through complex submerged conditions effortlessly.

2. **Hydrodynamic Productivity:**

The biomechanics of water launch add to the hydrodynamic effectiveness of squid impetus. The smoothed out state of the squid's body, related to the retractable blades, limits haul as water is ousted. The planned activity of roundabout and outspread muscles, joined with the unique control of the siphon, represents the hydrodynamic greatness that describes squid headway.

IV. Energetics of Water Discharge:

1. **Metabolic Requests:**
   The energetics of water discharge include contemplations of the metabolic requests related with the fast and powerful strong constrictions. Squids are profoundly dynamic hunters, and the energy use expected for supported fly drive is huge. The proficiency of water discharge becomes critical for adjusting the energy costs related with hunting, getting away from hunters, and different ways of behaving.

2. **Lightness Control:**

Water discharge likewise assumes a part in lightness control. By changing the power and length of mantle compressions, squids can control their situation in the water section. This lightness control is an extra part of the energetics of water discharge, as squids streamline their situation for different exercises, like hunting or keeping away from hunters.

V. Transformations for Proficient Push Age:

1. **Solid Design:**
   The productivity of water discharge is worked with by the specific strong engineering of squids. Round muscles create the underlying power for diminishing mantle pit volume, and outspread muscles add to the further decrease, improving the power of water removal. The planned activity of these muscles mirrors the transformation of water discharge for productive push age.

2. **Morphology of the Siphon:**
   The morphology of the siphon is adjusted for effective water ejection. The cylindrical design takes into consideration the quick and coordinated arrival of water, while its adaptability adds to the flexible spout impact. The powerful changes looking like the siphon, impacted by the constriction of mantle muscles, empower squids to control the bearing and power of water ejection with accuracy.

3. **Blades and Mantle Pipes:**

The association among balances and mantle withdrawal upgrades the effectiveness of pushed age. Blades, when withdrawn during strong mantle compressions, diminish drag and smooth out the squid's body. Mantle channels, structures related with the mantle, help with coordinating water stream. The organized developments of blades and mantle pipes add to the by and large hydrodynamic greatness of squid velocity.

VI. Social Parts of Pushed Age:

1. **Hunting and Prey Catch:**
   Push age through water discharge is a critical part of the hunting methodology utilized by squids. While hunting prey, squids use water launch to push themselves toward their objective quickly. The powerful ejection of water makes an eruption of speed, permitting squids to close the distance to their prey with accuracy. The capacity to control the course of water ejection upgrades their hunting achievement.
2. **Get away from Reactions:**

Push age is an essential piece of the squid's getaway reactions when confronted with possible dangers or hunters. The fast and powerful ejection of water empowers squids to execute equivocal moves, changing their position rapidly and escaping followers. This protective conduct features the flexibility and adaptability of pushed age in upgrading the endurance chances of squids.

VII. Biomimicry and Mechanical Advancement:

1. **Biomimetic Submerged Vehicles:**
   The job of water launch in creating push fills in as motivation for biomimetic applications in submerged innovation. Designers and specialists keen on working on the effectiveness of submerged vehicles, submarines, and independent submerged frameworks can draw experiences from the biomechanics of pushed age. Biomimetic submerged vehicles that recreate the customizable spout impact and hydrodynamic proficiency of squids can possibly improve dexterity and mobility in oceanic conditions.
2. **Impetus Frameworks:**
   The comprehension of the biomechanics and liquid elements of water launch offers important data for the improvement of more productive drive frameworks in human innovation. Specialists can investigate the standards of round and outspread muscle coordination, the flexible spout impact, and smoothed out morphology to plan impetus frameworks that imitate the productivity of cephalopod motion.
3. **Submerged Advanced mechanics:**

Biomimetic approaches enlivened by water launch have suggestions for the field of submerged advanced mechanics. Independent submerged vehicles intended to mirror the cadenced and strong mantle constrictions of squids could accomplish improved dexterity and accuracy in submerged investigation and reconnaissance. The biomimetic incorporation of customizable spouts could additionally add to the flexibility of these automated frameworks.

VIII. Difficulties and Future Headings:

1. **Copying Cadenced Withdrawals:**
   Reproducing the cadenced and facilitated withdrawals of round and outspread muscles represents a test in biomimetic applications. Accomplishing a consistent mix of these muscle activities in counterfeit frameworks requires a point by point comprehension of the brain control and biomechanics engaged with water launch.

2. **Materials and Adaptability:**
   Creating materials that imitate the adaptability and usefulness of the squid's mantle and siphon is a basic thought for biomimetic plans. Propels in materials science, including the production of engineered structures that can flex and agreement with comparable proficiency, are fundamental for effective biomimicry.

3. **Interdisciplinary Cooperation:**

The complete comprehension of the job of water discharge in producing push requires interdisciplinary joint effort between scholars, biomechanics specialists, liquid elements scientists, and designers. Future exploration headings ought to focus on cooperative endeavors to unwind the intricacies of squid movement and make an interpretation of these experiences into functional applications.

3.3 Research and Discoveries in Squid Propulsion Science

Examination and disclosures in squid impetus science have divulged a captivating domain of biomechanics, liquid elements, and regular designing. Researchers diving into the mysteries of cephalopod headway have taken critical steps in grasping the multifaceted components behind squid drive. Through thorough perception, high level imaging strategies, and biomechanical investigations, specialists have unraveled the coordinated movement of mantle constriction, siphon elements, and water discharge.

One striking advancement lies in the investigation of the neurological control systems overseeing squid impetus. Studies play uncovered the part of pacemaker cells and decentralized sensory systems in coordinating the musical compressions imperative for powerful fly drive. Furthermore, progressions in hydrodynamics research have revealed insight into the smoothed out morphology of squids, adding to their excellent dexterity in submerged conditions.

Besides, the field of biomimicry has been enormously affected by disclosures in squid impetus science. Engineers draw motivation from the customizable spout impact, roundabout and spiral muscle coordination, and the proficient water removal saw in squids to improve submerged advances, for example, biomimetic submerged vehicles and drive frameworks. The continuous exploration venture in squid drive science guarantees a more profound cognizance of cephalopod motion as well as thrilling possibilities for imaginative applications in submerged mechanical technology and impetus designing.

Chapter 4

Squid-inspired Technologies

The submerged domain, with its huge field and many-sided biological systems, has long enraptured the human creative mind. Among the natives of the profound, squids stand apart as magnificent pilots, utilizing an interesting plane drive framework for quick and spry development. Lately, researchers and architects have gone to these cephalopods for motivation, opening the insider facts of their impetus components to drive mechanical development. Squid-enlivened advances are arising as a promising outskirts, offering arrangements in fields going from mechanical technology to impetus frameworks. This investigation digs into the intriguing universe of squid-propelled advances, featuring key disclosures, biomimetic applications, and the groundbreaking effect on different ventures.

1. **Stream Drive Mysteries Revealed:**
1. **Biomechanics of Squid Impetus:**
   Understanding the biomechanics of squid impetus is fundamental to the improvement of squid-roused advances. Squids accomplish velocity through the fast withdrawal of roundabout and spiral muscles in their mantle, prompting the removal of water through a siphon. This activity response system, directed by standards of liquid elements and Newton's third regulation, moves squids with surprising effectiveness and accuracy.
2. **Neurological Bits of knowledge:**

Examination into the neurological control of squid impetus plays uncovered the part of pacemaker cells and the decentralized sensory system. The coordination between these components organizes the musical constrictions fundamental for successful fly impetus. Unwinding the brain complexities gives important experiences to reproducing squid-like motion in mechanical applications.

II. Biomimicry in Submerged Advanced mechanics:

1. **Movable Spout Impact:**
   The squid's siphon goes about as a customizable spout, empowering exact command over the bearing and power of water removal. In submerged mechanical technology, engineers are consolidating this customizable spout impact to upgrade the spryness and mobility of independent submerged vehicles (AUVs). Impersonating the squid's capacity to change the direction of its siphon, these biomimetic vehicles explore submerged conditions with more noteworthy adaptability.

2. **Hydrodynamically Effective Plans:**
   Squids brag a smoothed out morphology that limits haul during plane impetus. Biomimetic submerged vehicles draw motivation from this hydrodynamic effectiveness, taking on smooth plans that diminish opposition and work on in general execution. By copying the normal stream elements saw in squids, engineers expect to improve the effectiveness of submerged investigation and reconnaissance.

3. **Accuracy Route:**

Squid-propelled advancements add to accuracy route in submerged mechanical technology. The fast and controlled developments worked with by stream impetus components permit biomimetic vehicles to explore complex conditions with nimbleness. This ability is especially important in applications like marine exploration, submerged reviews, and search-and-salvage tasks.

III. Impetus Frameworks Enlivened by Squids:

1. **Proficient Water Launch:**
   The proficiency of water launch in squid impetus fills in as a model for the improvement of cutting edge drive frameworks. Engineers are investigating the standards of round and outspread muscle coordination, as well as the job of the guide, to plan impetus frameworks that copy the proficiency of cephalopod velocity. These frameworks hold guarantee for improving the exhibition of submerged vehicles and submarines.

2. **Lightness Control Components:**

Squids display exact lightness control through their fly impetus framework. Biomimetic approaches roused by squid lightness control are affecting the plan of submerged innovations that require exact profundity guideline. Subs and remotely worked vehicles (ROVs) are consolidating these components to streamline their situating in fluctuating water profundities.

IV. Materials Science and Squid-Roused Designs:

1. **Adaptable and Versatile Materials:**
   Squid mantles and siphons show exceptional adaptability during plane drive. Progresses in materials science mean to repeat this adaptability in engineered structures. Engineers are creating adaptable and versatile materials that emulate the biomechanical properties of squid tissues. These materials track down applications in the development of counterfeit siphons, upgrading the mobility and effectiveness of submerged vehicles.
2. **Imitating Strong Engineering:**

Squids have particular strong engineering, with roundabout and spiral muscles working couple for effective mantle compressions. Biomimetic advancements look to emulate this solid coordination in the improvement of fake muscles for drive frameworks. These engineered muscles, enlivened by the squid's regular plan, mean to upgrade the power and accuracy of submerged drive components.

V. Biomimetic Applications in Protection and Reconnaissance:

1. **Secrecy and Mobility:**
   The secrecy and mobility displayed by squids right at home move headways in guard and observation advancements. Biomimetic submerged vehicles planned with squid-like drive frameworks can explore covertly through water, making them ideal for observation missions. The capacity to quickly take a different path and limit unsettling influences in the water upgrades their viability in secret tasks.
2. **Independent Submerged Vehicles (AUVs):**

Squid-motivated innovations assume an essential part in the improvement of independent submerged vehicles. These AUVs, outfitted with biomimetic drive frameworks, display upgraded independence, spryness, and versatility. Applications range from submerged studies and natural checking to the reconnaissance of basic marine frameworks.

VI. Difficulties and Future Possibilities:

1. **Energy Proficiency Contemplations:**
   Notwithstanding the steps in squid-motivated advancements, challenges remain, especially in accomplishing energy productivity practically identical to regular frameworks. The metabolic requests related with the fast and strong compressions of squid mantle muscles present contemplations for the advancement of biomimetic drive frameworks. Analysts are investigating creative answers for offset effectiveness with energy use.
2. **Interdisciplinary Joint effort:**
   Squid-propelled advances require interdisciplinary coordinated effort between

scholars, biomechanics specialists, liquid elements analysts, materials researchers, and architects. Future headways depend on collaborations across these assorted fields to extend how we might interpret squid motion and make an interpretation of disclosures into pragmatic applications.

3. **Coordination of Man-made consciousness:**

The coordination of man-made consciousness (simulated intelligence) assumes a vital part in enhancing the presentation of squid-motivated advancements. Man-made intelligence calculations can improve the constant control and versatility of biomimetic submerged vehicles, permitting them to independently answer dynamic natural circumstances and explore complex landscapes.

4.1Overview of Existing Technologies Inspired by Squid Propulsion

Squids, with their momentous fly drive components, have filled in as a wellspring of motivation for mechanical development. The complex biomechanics of squid movement, described by fast mantle constrictions, water launch, and exact route, have prodded the advancement of different innovations across assorted fields. This outline investigates the current advancements propelled by squid impetus, crossing submerged mechanical technology, drive frameworks, materials science, and guard applications. From biomimetic submerged vehicles to adaptable materials impersonating squid structures, these advancements feature the groundbreaking capability of drawing from nature's designing wonders.

1. **Biomimetic Submerged Mechanical technology:**
1. **Flexible Spout Impact in Independent Submerged Vehicles (AUVs):**
   The squid's siphon, going about as a flexible spout, has motivated progressions in the plan of Independent Submerged Vehicles (AUVs). Biomimetic AUVs integrate customizable spouts that empower exact command over the bearing and power of water ejection, reflecting the squid's capacity to explore with dexterity. This innovation improves the mobility and adaptability of AUVs, making them ideal for errands like marine investigation, natural checking, and submerged observation.

2. **Hydrodynamically Productive Plans:**
   Squids' smoothed out morphology, upgraded for productive fly drive, has impacted the plan of biomimetic submerged robots. These robots take on smooth and hydrodynamically effective shapes, diminishing drag and working on generally execution. The utilization of squid-propelled hydrodynamics improves the proficiency of submerged robots, permitting them to explore through water with negligible obstruction.

3. **Accuracy Route in Biomimetic Vehicles:**

Squid-roused advances add to accuracy route in submerged mechanical technology. The quick and controlled developments worked with by fly drive components permit biomimetic vehicles to explore complex conditions with dexterity. This accuracy is especially important in applications like marine exploration, submerged assessments, and search-and-salvage activities, where the capacity to explore with precision is vital.

II. Impetus Frameworks Propelled by Squids:

1. **Proficient Water Launch for Improved Impetus:**
   The proficiency of water launch in squid drive has propelled the improvement of cutting edge impetus frameworks. Engineers are investigating the standards of round and outspread muscle coordination, as well as the job of the direct, to plan impetus frameworks that copy the effectiveness of cephalopod velocity. These frameworks hold guarantee for improving the exhibition of submerged vehicles, submarines, and remotely worked vehicles (ROVs) by giving effective and versatile method for impetus.

2. **Lightness Control Systems in Submarines:**

Squids show exact lightness control through their stream drive framework. Biomimetic approaches roused by squid lightness control have impacted the plan of subs and remotely worked vehicles. These advances consolidate systems that consider exact profundity guideline, empowering ideal situating in changing water profundities. The incorporation of squid-enlivened lightness control upgrades the productivity and versatility of submarine vehicles.

III. Materials Science and Squid-Roused Designs:

1. **Adaptable and Versatile Materials:**
   Squid mantles and siphons show astounding adaptability during plane drive. Progresses in materials science plan to reproduce this adaptability in engineered structures. Engineers are creating adaptable and versatile materials that imitate the biomechanical properties of squid tissues. These materials track down applications in the development of counterfeit siphons, improving the mobility and proficiency of submerged vehicles. Squid-propelled adaptable materials add to the advancement of stronger and versatile designs in different designing applications.

2. **Imitating Solid Engineering for Impetus:**

Squids have specific solid engineering, with round and spiral muscles working pair for effective mantle compressions. Biomimetic advancements try to mirror this solid coordination in the improvement of counterfeit muscles for drive frameworks. These manufactured muscles, propelled by the squid's regular plan, intend to upgrade the power and accuracy of submerged drive components. The use of squid-propelled solid design adds to the advancement of more effective and biomimetic actuators in mechanical technology and designing.

IV. Biomimetic Applications in Guard and Observation:

1. **Covertness and Mobility in Protection Advances:**
   Squid-enlivened advances have tracked down applications in safeguard, where covertness and mobility are basic. Biomimetic submerged vehicles planned with squid-like impetus frameworks can explore subtly through water, making them ideal for reconnaissance missions. The capacity to quickly take an alternate route and limit aggravations in the water improves their viability in secret tasks. These advancements add to progressions in submerged protection frameworks and vital reconnaissance.

2. **Independent Submerged Vehicles (AUVs) in Safeguard:**

   Squid-roused innovations assume a vital part in the improvement of Independent Submerged Vehicles (AUVs) for protection applications. These AUVs, outfitted with biomimetic drive frameworks, show upgraded independence, deftness, and versatility. Guard applications incorporate submerged reviews, observing vital sea areas, and leading secret insight tasks. Squid-propelled AUVs give a significant device to guard powers to explore and assemble basic data in testing submerged conditions.

V. Difficulties and Future Possibilities:

1. **Energy Productivity Contemplations in Biomimetic Advancements:**
   Regardless of the headways in squid-propelled advancements, challenges continue, especially in accomplishing energy effectiveness similar to normal frameworks. The metabolic requests related with the fast and strong compressions of squid mantle muscles present contemplations for the advancement of biomimetic impetus frameworks. Analysts are investigating creative answers for offset effectiveness with energy consumption, trying to upgrade the presentation of biomimetic advancements.

2. **Interdisciplinary Joint effort for Proceeded with Advancement:**
   Squid-enlivened innovations require interdisciplinary cooperation between scholars, biomechanics specialists, liquid elements analysts, materials researchers, and designers. Future progressions depend on collaborations across these assorted fields to extend how we might interpret squid motion and make an interpretation of disclosures into pragmatic applications. Proceeded with joint effort will cultivate the advancement of more refined and proficient squid-roused innovations.

3. **Incorporation of Man-made brainpower for Improvement:**

The combination of man-made brainpower (artificial intelligence) assumes a critical part in upgrading the presentation of squid-roused innovations. Simulated intelligence calculations can improve the constant control and flexibility of biomimetic submerged vehicles, permitting them to independently answer dynamic natural circumstances and explore complex landscapes. The utilization of computer based intelligence related to squid-motivated drive frameworks opens roads for additional development and improvement.

4.2 Robotics and Underwater Vehicles

The investigation of the submerged world has consistently introduced one of a kind difficulties because of the cruel circumstances and the restrictions forced by human physiology. In light of these difficulties, advanced mechanics and submerged vehicles have arisen as noteworthy innovations, changing our capacity to study, overview, and explore the tremendous scopes of the sea. This outline digs into the groundbreaking effect of mechanical technology and submerged vehicles, investigating their assorted applications, mechanical headways, and the job they play in growing comprehension we might interpret the sea's secrets.

1. **Investigation and Logical Exploration:**
1. **Independent Submerged Vehicles (AUVs):**
   Independent Submerged Vehicles, or AUVs, address a change in outlook in submerged investigation. These automated vehicles are furnished with sensors and navigational frameworks, empowering them to work independently, gather information, and communicate data progressively. AUVs have been instrumental in logical exploration, permitting specialists to concentrate on marine biological systems, map the sea depths, and examine submerged land highlights. Their independence and flexibility make AUVs important instruments for sea life researcher, oceanographers, and ecological researchers.
2. **Remote Worked Vehicles (ROVs):**

Remote Worked Vehicles, or ROVs, are fastened automated gadgets constrained by human administrators on a superficial level. ROVs are pivotal for undertakings that require human mediation, like remote ocean investigation, oil and gas industry tasks, and archeological overviews. With cutting edge imaging situation and controller arms, ROVs can arrive at profundities past the abilities of human jumpers, giving exceptional admittance to the sea's profundities.

II. Submerged Mechanical technology in Industry:

1. **Subsea Assessments and Support:**
   The modern area has embraced submerged mechanical technology for subsea investigations and upkeep. ROVs furnished with superior quality cameras and specific sensors can assess submerged designs, pipelines, and seaward

establishments. This application limits the requirement for exorbitant and tedious human mediations, guaranteeing the effective and safe activity of lowered foundation in businesses like oil and gas, sustainable power, and broadcast communications.

2. **Submerged Development and Fix:**

Submerged mechanical technology is progressively used for development and fix assignments in testing submerged conditions. ROVs furnished with cutting devices, welding capacities, and controller arms can perform many-sided errands, for example, pipeline fixes, link establishments, and submerged framework development. These applications upgrade the productivity and wellbeing of submerged development projects, decreasing the dangers related with human jumpers working in unfriendly circumstances.

III. Ecological Observing and Protection:

1. **Marine Environment Studies:**
   Mechanical technology and submerged vehicles assume an imperative part in marine environment studies, offering a non-nosy means to notice and screen marine life. AUVs furnished with natural sensors can gather information on water temperature, saltiness, and compound organization, adding to how we might interpret sea elements. These innovations empower researchers to concentrate on transient examples, screen biodiversity, and survey the effect of natural changes on marine environments.

2. **Contamination Observation:**

Submerged mechanical technology is conveyed for contamination observation and reaction endeavors. AUVs furnished with sensors can recognize and follow poisons, oil slicks, and other natural dangers. This capacity is urgent for quick reaction and alleviating the biological effect of contamination occurrences. Submerged vehicles add to ecological protection by giving significant information to policymakers, researchers, and preservationists.

IV. Innovative Headways:

1. **Scaling down and Sensor Reconciliation:**
   Mechanical headways in scaling down and sensor reconciliation have fundamentally improved the abilities of submerged mechanical technology. Smaller than expected AUVs outfitted with cutting edge sensors can explore restricted spaces, investigate many-sided submerged landscape, and catch high-goal information. Sensor incorporation permits these vehicles to gather a large number of ecological information, adding to additional exhaustive investigations of submerged environments.

2. Computerized reasoning and Independence:

The joining of man-made consciousness (artificial intelligence) and independence has changed the field of submerged mechanical technology. AUVs and ROVs outfitted with computer based intelligence calculations can settle on continuous choices, adjust to changing natural circumstances, and upgrade their route courses. This degree of independence improves the proficiency and responsiveness of submerged vehicles, making them more versatile to dynamic and capricious submerged conditions.

V. Difficulties and Future Bearings:

1. **Energy Productivity and Perseverance:**
Energy productivity and perseverance stay critical difficulties for submerged mechanical technology. Creating power-productive impetus frameworks and energy stockpiling arrangements is vital for broadening the functional span of AUVs and ROVs. Advancements in sustainable power sources, for example, submerged charging stations and energy gathering advancements, hold guarantee for tending to these difficulties.

2. **Correspondence and Information Transmission:**
Correspondence and information transmission in submerged conditions present extraordinary difficulties because of restricted perceivability and sign lessening. Headways in acoustic correspondence advances, submerged remote organizations, and constant information transmission are fundamental for working on the network and correspondence capacities of submerged mechanical technology.

3. **Interdisciplinary Joint effort:**

The proceeded with headway of submerged advanced mechanics requires interdisciplinary coordinated effort between engineers, sea life researchers, PC researchers, and materials researchers. Consolidating ability in mechanical technology, sea life science, and man-made intelligence will prompt the improvement of more modern, versatile, and ecologically cognizant submerged advances.

4.3 Aerospace and Aircraft Design

The field of aviation and airplane configuration remains at the bleeding edge of mechanical development, forming the manner in which mankind navigates the skies. From the Wright siblings' notable trip to the state of the art progressions in current flying, the development of airplane configuration has been a demonstration of human resourcefulness and designing ability. This exhaustive outline digs into the complexities of advanced plane design, investigating the standards of airplane plan, innovative leap forwards, challenges looked by the business, and what's in store prospects that lie ahead.

1. **Essentials of Airplane Plan:**
1. **Optimal design:**
   Streamlined features shapes the groundwork of airplane configuration, zeroing in on the investigation of wind current around an airplane's surfaces. Wings, fuselage, and control surfaces are carefully molded to upgrade lift, lessen drag, and guarantee stable flight. Standards, for example, Bernoulli's condition and the Coanda impact guide engineers in creating efficiently productive airplane.

2. **Foundational layout:**
   The underlying trustworthiness of an airplane is fundamental for security and execution. Engineers utilize materials like aluminum, titanium, and high level composites to plan lightweight yet strong airframes. Limited Component Investigation (FEA) and stress examination procedures guarantee that the airplane's construction can endure the powers experienced during flight, including disturbance, moves, and arrivals.

3. **Drive Frameworks:**
   Drive frameworks, like fly motors and propellers, are essential to airplane plan. Fly motors work on the guideline of pushed produced by the launch of rapid exhaust gases, while propellers influence the turn of sharp edges to drive the airplane forward. The decision of drive framework relies upon factors like airplane size, planned use, and productivity necessities.

4. **Aeronautics and Control Frameworks:**

Aeronautics includes the electronic frameworks that control and screen airplane activities. Flight control frameworks, autopilots, route frameworks, and correspondence hardware depend on cutting edge gadgets and programming. The combination of sensors, gyrators, and complex control calculations guarantees exact and stable flight, adding to the security and proficiency of airplane activities.

II. Authentic Achievements in Airplane Plan:

1. **Wright Siblings' Flyer (1903):**
   The Wright siblings, Orville and Wilbur, accomplished a memorable achievement with the first fueled, controlled, and supported trip of the Wright Flyer on December 17, 1903. This biplane highlighted a wingspan of 40 feet, a 12.3-drive motor, and a three-hub control framework. The outcome of the Wright Flyer denoted the introduction of present day aeronautics.

2. **Soul of St. Louis (1927):**
   Charles Lindbergh's relentless independent transoceanic trip in the Soul of St. Louis exhibited the capability of long-range flight. The airplane, a uniquely constructed monoplane, stressed eco-friendliness and reach, permitting Lindbergh to finish the noteworthy excursion from New York to Paris. This achievement prodded headways in significant distance air travel.

3. **Stream Age and the Boeing 707 (1958):**
   The Boeing 707 denoted the start of the Stream Age, presenting business fly travel for an enormous scope. Fly motors gave higher paces, expanded proficiency, and decreased travel times. The 707's prosperity reformed air transportation, making air travel more open and productive for travelers all over the planet.
4. **Space Age and the Space Transport (1981):**

The Space Transport, addressed by NASA's Space Transportation Framework (STS), was an earth shattering improvement in aviation. Consolidating a spaceplane orbiter, strong rocket supporters, and an outside gas tank, the Space Transport empowered reusable spaceflight. It assumed a significant part in different space missions, including satellite send-offs and space station gathering.

III. Mechanical Progressions in Aviation:

1. **Fly-by-Wire Frameworks:**
   Fly-by-wire frameworks supplanted conventional mechanical control frameworks with electronic partners. These frameworks use sensors to distinguish pilot input, which is then sent to control surfaces through electronic signs. Fly-by-wire upgrades airplane mobility, productivity, and wellbeing, considering PC helped control and computerization.
2. **Composite Materials:**
   High level composite materials, for example, carbon-fiber-supported polymers, have altered airplane development. These lightweight and high-strength materials offer better eco-friendliness, underlying uprightness, and protection from weakness. Present day airplane, including the Boeing 787 Dreamliner and Airbus A350, widely use composites in their airframes.
3. **Secrecy Innovation:**
   Secrecy innovation expects to diminish an airplane's radar cross-segment, making it less perceptible by adversary radar frameworks. Airplane like the Lockheed Martin F-22 Raptor and F-35 Lightning II component covertness plan components, including mixed wing-body designs and radar-engrossing materials, upgrading their survivability in threatening conditions.
4. **Supersonic and Hypersonic Flight:**

Headways in impetus and streamlined features have reignited interest in supersonic and hypersonic flight. The Concorde, a supersonic traveler stream, worked from 1976 to 2003, exhibiting the plausibility of rapid air travel. Progressing innovative work in hypersonic flight plan to accomplish speeds surpassing Mach 5, with expected applications in military and space investigation.

IV. Challenges in Airplane Plan:

1. **Ecological Effect:**
   The ecological effect of avionics, especially fossil fuel byproducts and commotion contamination, presents critical difficulties. Airplane makers and scientists are investigating elective energizes, electric impetus frameworks, and economical plan practices to moderate the natural impression of flight.

2. **Eco-friendliness and Reach:**
   Improving eco-friendliness and broadening the scope of airplane are continuous needs. High level streamlined features, lightweight materials, and further developed motor advancements add to accomplishing more prominent eco-friendliness. The improvement of mixture and electric drive frameworks is likewise investigating new roads for manageable flight.

3. **Security and Computerization:**
   While robotization improves flight security, it likewise presents difficulties connected with human-machine collaboration and possible over-dependence on mechanized frameworks. Guaranteeing that pilots are thoroughly prepared to deal with manual tasks during crises is basic for keeping a harmony among robotization and human intercession.

4. **Administrative Consistence:**

Airplane configuration should conform to severe wellbeing and administrative principles set by flight specialists around the world. Fulfilling these guidelines while consolidating inventive advances and plans requires close joint effort between producers, controllers, and industry partners.

V. Future Bearings and Advancements:

1. **Metropolitan Air Versatility (UAM):**
   Metropolitan Air Portability imagines the utilization of little electric vertical departure and landing (eVTOL) airplane for brief distance metropolitan transportation. These vehicles, frequently alluded to as air taxis, expect to ease gridlock and give productive elevated transportation inside urban areas. Organizations like Uber and aviation new companies are effectively investigating UAM ideas.

2. **Electric and Hydrogen-Controlled Airplane:**
   Electric and hydrogen-fueled airplane address a promising road for feasible flying. Organizations are creating electric drive frameworks and investigating the attainability of hydrogen energy units to control airplane, planning to diminish dependence on customary petroleum products and limit fossil fuel byproducts.

3. **Independent Airplane:**
   The advancement of independent airplane, equipped for self-steering and exploring without human mediation, is a developing outskirts in aviation. While full independence in business flight is a drawn out objective, gradual advances,

like independent navigating and landing, are being investigated to improve proficiency and wellbeing.

4. **High level Materials and Assembling Methods:**

Proceeded with headways in materials science and assembling procedures are molding the fate of airplane plan. Added substance fabricating (3D printing), for example, considers complicated and lightweight part creation. New materials with improved solidarity to-weight proportions add to more proficient and eco-accommodating airplane.

Chapter 5

Challenges And Future Prospects

The domain of aviation and airplane configuration isn't without its difficulties, and as innovation keeps on advancing, new open doors and intricacies arise. This exhaustive investigation digs into the difficulties looked by the avionic business and imagines what's to come prospects that anticipate. From natural worries to mechanical developments, the way forward is both testing and loaded up with potential for earth shattering progressions.

1. **Ecological Difficulties:**
1. **Fossil fuel byproducts:**
   One of the essential difficulties standing up to the airplane business is the natural effect of fossil fuel byproducts from airplane. Customary flying fills add to ozone depleting substance emanations, adding to environmental change. As the interest for air head out keeps on developing, addressing fossil fuel byproducts becomes basic to guarantee a maintainable and earth capable flight area.
2. **Commotion Contamination:**

One more ecological test is commotion contamination created via airplane during departure, landing, and flight. Networks around air terminals are unfavorably impacted by the commotion, prompting worries about wellbeing and prosperity. Finding some kind of harmony between proficient air travel and alleviating commotion contamination requires creative methodologies in airplane plan and functional practices.

II. Eco-friendliness and Practical Flight:

1. **Further developing Eco-friendliness:**
   Improving eco-friendliness is an unending objective in airplane plan. Fuel addresses a critical functional expense for carriers, and upgrading airplane for better eco-friendliness straightforwardly influences both monetary and natural maintainability. High level streamlined features, lightweight materials, and

creative impetus frameworks add to accomplishing higher eco-friendliness in present day airplane.

2. **Elective Energizes:**

The journey for feasible flight has prompted the investigation of elective fills. Biofuels got from sustainable sources, for example, green growth or waste materials, offer a likely answer for diminish the carbon impression of flight. Furthermore, progressing investigation into engineered fills and hydrogen-controlled drive frameworks holds guarantee for changing the flying business into a more maintainable venture.

III. Security and Mechanization:

1. **Robotization Difficulties:**
   While robotization improves the wellbeing and productivity of air travel, it acquaints difficulties related with human-machine collaboration and possible over-dependence on computerized frameworks. Guaranteeing that pilots are satisfactorily prepared to deal with manual activities during crises is basic. Finding some kind of harmony among robotization and human mediation is a continuous test in airplane plan.

2. **Human Variables:**

Human elements, enveloping the mental and physiological parts of human execution, assume an essential part in flight security. Planning cockpit connection points, controls, and shows that streamline pilot direction and diminish the gamble of blunders requires a profound comprehension of human elements. As airplane become all the more innovatively progressed, tending to human elements turns out to be progressively perplexing.

IV. Administrative Consistence:

1. **Rigid Security Guidelines:**
   Meeting rigid security and administrative guidelines is quite difficult for airplane creators and producers. Administrative bodies overall set thorough norms to guarantee the security of air travel. The advancing idea of innovation, combined with the requirement for advancement, requires a cooperative exertion between the avionic business and administrative specialists to create and carry out norms that focus on wellbeing.

2. **Worldwide Harmonization:**

Accomplishing worldwide harmonization in avionics guidelines is a continuous test. Contrasts in administrative systems among nations and areas can present snags to worldwide participation and the consistent mix of new advancements. Laying out normal guidelines that are acknowledged universally is essential for encouraging a durable and productive aviation environment.

V. Innovative Headways:

1. **Electric and Cross breed Drive:**
   The turn of events and joining of electric and mixture drive frameworks address a mechanical outskirts in aviation. Electric airplane, driven by electric engines or cross breed frameworks consolidating conventional and electric impetus, can possibly diminish fossil fuel byproducts and improve eco-friendliness. Conquering difficulties connected with energy capacity, weight contemplations, and foundation improvement is fundamental for the broad reception of electric impetus.

2. **High level Materials and Assembling:**
   Propels in materials science and assembling methods keep on molding the scene of airplane plan. Added substance fabricating (3D printing) considers the creation of mind boggling and lightweight parts, adding to eco-friendliness. The improvement of cutting edge materials with better strength-than weight proportions upgrades the underlying honesty of airplane while decreasing by and large weight.

3. **Metropolitan Air Portability (UAM):**

Metropolitan Air Portability (UAM) imagines the joining of little electric vertical departure and landing (eVTOL) airplane into metropolitan transportation organizations. This groundbreaking idea presents innovative difficulties connected with sound decrease, foundation improvement, and the coordination of air traffic the board frameworks. Understanding the maximum capacity of UAM requires conquering these obstacles and laying out an administrative system that guarantees wellbeing and effectiveness.

VI. Future Possibilities and Advancements:

1. **Hydrogen-Controlled Airplane:**
   Hydrogen-fueled airplane address a cutting edge prospect for maintainable flight. Hydrogen energy units, which produce power through the response of hydrogen with oxygen, offer a perfect and proficient option in contrast to customary flight fills. Innovative work endeavors are in progress to investigate the achievability of hydrogen-controlled impetus frameworks and address difficulties connected with capacity, appropriation, and foundation.

2. **Independent Airplane:**
   The fate of flight incorporates the improvement of independent airplane equipped for self-guiding and exploring without human mediation. While full independence in business flight is a drawn out objective, gradual advances,

like independent navigating and landing, are being investigated to upgrade proficiency and wellbeing. Defeating administrative, mechanical, and public acknowledgment difficulties will be critical to acknowledging independent flight.

3. **Supersonic and Hypersonic Travel:**
Supersonic and hypersonic travel are areas of continuous innovative work, expecting to upset significant distance air travel. Supersonic airplane, going at speeds surpassing Mach 1, and hypersonic airplane, surpassing Mach 5, present difficulties connected with streamlined features, materials, and drive. The improvement of these high velocity innovations could fundamentally decrease travel times and open additional opportunities for worldwide network.

4. **Ecological Maintainability Drives:**

Future possibilities in aviation are intently attached to ecological maintainability drives. The business is effectively investigating ways of lessening its carbon impression, take on reasonable practices, and embrace round economy standards. Cooperative endeavors between industry partners, state run administrations, and natural associations are essential for accomplishing significant advancement in moderating the ecological effect of flying.

5.1Current Challenges in Applying Squid Propulsion to Technology

Squid impetus, with its wonderful productivity and accuracy, has dazzled specialists and designers looking for inventive answers for submerged innovation. The capacity of squids to quickly push themselves utilizing plane impetus has enlivened the advancement of biomimetic innovations. Notwithstanding, interpreting the complicated biomechanics of squid velocity into down to earth applications presents a bunch of difficulties. This far reaching investigation digs into the flow moves looked in applying squid impetus to innovation, tending to the intricacies associated with impersonating nature's submerged wonder.

1. **Biomechanical Intricacy:**
1. **Emulating Mantle Withdrawal:**
Squid drive depends on the fast constriction of the mantle, a solid design that removes water through a siphon, producing forward push. Repeating this biomechanical intricacy in fake frameworks presents difficulties in planning actuators and systems that can emulate the exact and strong mantle withdrawals of squids. Accomplishing a harmony between speed, power, and productivity stays an imposing undertaking.

2. **Coordination of Solid Developments:**

Squids show a complex coordination of round and spiral muscles during drive. The mind boggling coordination of solid developments guarantees the controlled ejection of water for exact route. Emulating this coordination in fake frameworks requires progressed control calculations and activation advances to imitate the liquid and amicable developments saw in squids.

II. Energy Productivity Contemplations:

1. **Metabolic Requests and Energy Consumption:**
   Squid drive is innately energy-proficient, permitting these cephalopods to explore their submerged surroundings quickly. Nonetheless, reproducing this productivity in biomimetic advancements presents difficulties regarding energy consumption. The fast and strong mantle withdrawals request a cautious harmony among power and energy utilization, particularly in applications where drawn out activity is fundamental.

2. **Advancing Biomimetic Frameworks:**

Accomplishing energy effectiveness in biomimetic frameworks roused by squid drive requires a careful comprehension of the metabolic requests related with normal movement. Analysts face the test of streamlining counterfeit frameworks to imitate the proficiency of squids while limiting energy utilization. Imaginative arrangements in materials, activation, and configuration are important to find some kind of harmony.

III. Hydrodynamics and Liquid Elements:

1. **Smoothed out Shape and Hydrodynamic Plan:**
   Squids show a smoothed out and hydrodynamic shape that limits drag and upgrades drive productivity. Imitating this shape in biomimetic submerged vehicles is urgent for accomplishing ideal execution. In any case, the interpretation of hydrodynamic standards from nature to innovation requires a profound comprehension of liquid elements, materials science, and designing plan to make proficient and flexibility vehicles.

2. **Mobility and Accuracy:**

Squids grandstand striking mobility and accuracy in their impetus, permitting them to explore complex submerged conditions with dexterity. Imitating these abilities in biomimetic frameworks requires headways in control frameworks and route calculations. Defeating the difficulties of accuracy control in unique submerged conditions is fundamental for the fruitful utilization of squid-roused impetus.

IV. Materials Science and Underlying Difficulties:

1. **Adaptable and Versatile Materials:**
   Squid mantles and siphons display a serious level of adaptability and strength during plane drive. Biomimetic advances expecting to recreate this adaptability face difficulties in materials science. Creating engineered materials that can

imitate the mechanical properties of squid tissues while enduring submerged conditions represents a huge test.

2. **Underlying Honesty and Strength:**

The submerged climate is brutal, exposing materials to erosion, pressure, and bio-fouling. Squid-motivated advances should address primary uprightness and solidness difficulties to guarantee dependable activity in assorted marine conditions. Propels in materials designing, erosion safe coatings, and against fouling advancements are basic for the drawn out feasibility of squid-roused frameworks.

V. Tangible Mix and Independence:

1. **Coordination of Tangible Frameworks:**
   Squids depend on a blend of visual, material, and hydrodynamic tangible data to explore and chase. Integrating comparable tangible abilities into biomimetic advancements is trying because of the intricacies of sensor coordination sub-merged. Creating vigorous and proficient tangible frameworks that can copy the squid's capacity to detect and answer the climate is an ongoing obstacle in the utilization of squid impetus.

2. **Independent Route in Unique Conditions:**

Squids exhibit independent route in unique submerged conditions, adjusting their developments in view of continuous tactile info. Copying this degree of independence in counterfeit frameworks requires modern calculations for discernment, direction, and control. Exploring through testing submerged landscapes while answering natural changes stays a huge test in the use of squid-roused drive.

VI. Interdisciplinary Cooperation:

1. **Researcher, Specialists, and Material Researchers Cooperation:**
   Effective execution of squid drive in innovation requires interdisciplinary co-operation between scholars, specialists, and material researchers. Overcoming any barrier between understanding the organic systems in squids and making an interpretation of that information into commonsense applications requires a cooperative methodology. Defeating language and strategy contrasts between disciplines is significant for propelling squid-enlivened advancements.

2. **Liquid Elements and Control Frameworks Mix:**

Liquid elements scientists and control frameworks engineers should team up near advance the exhibition of squid-propelled impetus. Coordinating liquid elements standards into the plan of control frameworks presents difficulties regarding continu-ous versatility and responsiveness. Interdisciplinary coordinated effort is fundamental for creating consistent joining between liquid elements and control frameworks.

VII. Cost and Adaptability:

1. **Cost of Biomimetic Innovations:**
   Creating biomimetic innovations roused by squid impetus includes examination, trial and error, and the development of particular materials and parts. The expense related with these cycles represents a test for far and wide reception. Analysts and designers should investigate practical assembling techniques without compromising the quality and execution of squid-motivated frameworks.
2. **Versatility for Functional Applications:**

The versatility of squid-enlivened impetus for down to earth applications is a basic thought. While research center examinations and models feature the attainability of the innovation, increasing for certifiable situations, like submerged investigation, reconnaissance, or ecological observing, requires addressing difficulties connected with size, weight, and functional productivity.

VIII. Moral and Natural Worries:

1. **Influence on Marine Environments:**
   The organization of squid-enlivened advances in regular marine conditions raises moral and natural worries. The likely effect on marine environments, including disturbance to neighborhood fauna and verdure, requires cautious thought. Scientists should assess the biological outcomes of presenting fake frameworks that copy normal ways of behaving.
2. **Mindful Plan and Arrangement:**

Moral contemplations stretch out to the mindful plan, sending, and removal of squid-enlivened advances. Scientists and specialists are tested to stick to standards of manageability, limiting any adverse consequences on the climate. Executing thorough moral rules and natural effect evaluations is critical for the capable use of squid drive to innovation.

IX. Public Insight and Acknowledgment:

1. **Understanding and Trust:**
   The fruitful joining of squid-motivated impetus into innovation depends on open comprehension and trust. Instructing the general population about the advantages, applications, and moral contemplations related with biomimetic innovations is fundamental. Building a positive insight and addressing concerns connected with the natural and moral ramifications of squid-motivated frameworks is a continuous test.
2. **Correspondence and Effort:**

Scientists and designers face the test of successful correspondence and effort to gather public help. Straightforward correspondence about the goals, limits, and expected advantages of squid-roused innovations is fundamental for encouraging acknowledgment. Drawing in with networks, policymakers, and natural gatherings can add to an additional educated and strong public.

5.2 Ongoing Research and Development Efforts

The interest with the biomechanics of squid drive has prodded a flood of continuous innovative work endeavors pointed toward outfitting the mysteries of these cephalopods for mechanical applications. As scientists dig further into the intricacies of squid headway, they look to make an interpretation of their discoveries into imaginative answers for submerged investigation, advanced mechanics, and ecological checking. This thorough investigation dives into the present status of progressing innovative work endeavors in squid impetus innovation, revealing insight into the thrilling headways, difficulties, and future possibilities.

1. **Biomechanical Experiences and Biomimicry:**

1. **Grasping Squid Motion:**
   Progressing research attempts center around disentangling the complexities of squid movement, diving into the biomechanics of mantle withdrawals, water removal through siphons, and the job of balances in controlling. Propels in imaging innovations, like high velocity cameras and hydrodynamic reproductions, add to a more nuanced comprehension of how squids accomplish effective and exact impetus.

2. **Biomimetic Plans:**

Analysts are effectively taken part in making an interpretation of biomechanical bits of knowledge into biomimetic plans. The objective is to reproduce the vital components of squid impetus, including mantle compressions, siphon elements, and blade developments, in counterfeit frameworks. Biomimetic submerged vehicles and robots motivated by squids are being created, meaning to impersonate the effectiveness and dexterity saw in nature.

II. Materials Science and Delicate Mechanical technology:

1. **Adaptable and Strong Materials:**
   Materials science assumes a significant part in continuous exploration endeavors, with an emphasis on creating adaptable and strong materials that emulate the properties of squid tissues. Delicate mechanical technology, a field that underlines the utilization of consistent and deformable materials, is acquiring noticeable quality in the journey to repeat the normal developments of squids. Progresses in delicate advanced mechanics add to the formation of counterfeit frameworks that can deftly move submerged.

2. **Elastomeric Actuators:**

Elastomeric actuators, propelled by the flexibility of squid muscles, are a subject of progressing research. These actuators are intended to contract and grow like normal muscle tissue, giving a biomimetic way to deal with impetus. Scientists investigate different elastomeric materials and incitation instruments to accomplish the powerful developments expected for successful squid-propelled impetus.

III. Hydrodynamics and Computational Demonstrating:

1. **Hydrodynamic Standards:**
   Continuous examination dives into the hydrodynamic standards basic squid impetus. Computational demonstrating, liquid elements reenactments, and tests in water tanks add to a more profound comprehension of how squids upgrade their shape and developments for proficient swimming. Hydrodynamic experiences illuminate the plan regarding biomimetic frameworks to guarantee ideal execution in different submerged conditions.

2. **Enhancing Drive Effectiveness:**

Computational displaying permits scientists to improve the impetus effectiveness of biomimetic frameworks. By dissecting the associations between counterfeit blades or propulsive designs and water, scientists can adjust plans to limit drag, upgrade push, and work on generally speaking effectiveness. These recreations guide the iterative improvement of squid-motivated innovations.

IV. Energy Productivity and Independence:

1. **Energy Gathering Innovations:**
   Accomplishing energy productivity in fake frameworks roused by squid drive is a point of convergence of continuous examination. Specialists investigate energy gathering innovations, including systems that convert water stream or development into electrical energy. This approach means to diminish the dependence on outside power sources, making squid-roused advancements more reasonable and independent.

2. **Independent Route Calculations:**

Progressing research endeavors center around the improvement of independent route calculations for squid-enlivened advancements. These calculations empower counterfeit frameworks to adjust to dynamic submerged conditions, answer tactile info, and pursue constant choices. Accomplishing a harmony among independence and human control is fundamental for the down to earth use of squid-roused drive in different situations.

V. Tactile Incorporation and Bio-Roused Sensors:

1. **Bio-Roused Sensors:**
Squids depend on a modern exhibit of sensors, including visual and material organs, to explore their environmental factors. Continuous examination investigates the combination of bio-motivated sensors into counterfeit frameworks, improving their capacity to detect and answer submerged conditions. These sensors add to the advancement of more versatile and setting mindful squid-enlivened innovations.
2. **Coordination of Different Tangible Modalities:**

Impersonating the tangible joining saw in squids, scientists are dealing with coordinating different tactile modalities into counterfeit frameworks. Consolidating visual, material, and hydrodynamic sensors permits biomimetic innovations to assemble exhaustive data about the submerged climate. This multisensory approach upgrades the situational mindfulness and responsiveness of squid-motivated frameworks.

VI. Interdisciplinary Joint efforts:

1. **Scholars, Specialists, and Mechanical technology Specialists Coordinated effort:**
Continuous exploration endeavors underline interdisciplinary coordinated efforts between scientists, architects, and advanced mechanics specialists. Researcher give bits of knowledge into the organic components of squid impetus, engineers make an interpretation of these experiences into mechanical arrangements, and advanced mechanics specialists contribute mastery in control frameworks and computerization. Cooperative undertakings overcome any barrier between organic comprehension and mechanical application.
2. **Cross-Disciplinary Preparation Projects:**

To encourage cooperation and cross-disciplinary advancement, research establishments are progressively executing preparing programs that unite scientists from different fields. Cross-disciplinary preparation programs empower scientists to acquire experiences into designing standards as well as the other way around, making a common information base that speeds up progress in squid drive innovation.

VII. Genuine Applications and Field Testing:

1. **Submerged Advanced mechanics and Investigation:**
Progressing research stretches out past lab examinations to genuine applications, with an emphasis on submerged mechanical technology and investigation. Squid-motivated submerged vehicles are being produced for errands like ecological observing, marine exploration, and submerged observation. Field testing permits specialists to survey the exhibition and versatility of biomimetic advances in normal submerged conditions.

2. **Natural Observing and Observation:**

Squid-roused advancements show guarantee in applications connected with natural observing and reconnaissance. Submerged vehicles furnished with biomimetic impetus frameworks can explore testing landscapes and assemble information for ecological appraisals. These innovations add to endeavors pointed toward understanding and saving marine biological systems.

VIII. Difficulties and Future Bearings:

1. **Challenges in Increasing:**
   Notwithstanding critical advancement, challenges in increasing squid-enlivened advancements for down to earth applications endure. Scientists are effectively resolving issues connected with size, weight, and functional productivity to guarantee that biomimetic frameworks are practical for a scope of submerged applications.

2. **Natural and Moral Contemplations:**

Continuous examination stresses the significance of natural and moral contemplations. Scientists are attempting to survey the likely effect of squid-propelled advancements on marine environments, executing capable plan rehearses and taking into account the moral ramifications of conveying fake frameworks in regular habitats.

IX. Worldwide Cooperation and Information Sharing:

1. **Worldwide Exploration Organizations:**
   To propel the field of squid impetus innovation, global coordinated effort and information sharing are fundamental. Worldwide examination networks work with the trading of discoveries, systems, and best works on, permitting analysts from various districts to add to and benefit from progressing headways.

2. **Open-Access Stages and Data sets:**

The foundation of open-access stages and data sets improves the availability of examination results in squid drive innovation. Sharing information, reproductions, and exploratory outcomes on open-access stages cultivates a cooperative and straightforward examination climate, speeding up progress and limiting overt repetitiveness in research endeavors.

5.3 Potential Breakthroughs and Innovations on the Horizon

The domain of squid impetus innovation is near the very edge of extraordinary forward leaps and developments, driven by a combination of organic bits of knowledge, designing ability, and a guarantee to practical arrangements. As scientists keep on unwinding the secrets of squid headway, the skyline is abounding with potential progressions that could change submerged investigation, mechanical technology, and ecological observing. This investigation digs into the expected forward leaps and advancements not too far off in squid impetus innovation, revealing insight into the thrilling prospects that might shape the fate of this blossoming field.

1. **High level Materials for Biomimicry:**
1. **Bio-Propelled Materials with Self-Recuperating Properties:**
   The skyline holds the commitment of bio-propelled materials with self-recuperating properties, impersonating the regenerative capacities saw in squid tissues. Analysts are investigating materials that can independently fix harm brought about by natural factors or mileage. This advancement could upgrade the solidness and life span of squid-motivated innovations, making them stronger in submerged conditions.
2. **Savvy Materials for Versatile Disguise:**

Squids are famous for their capacity to change tone and surface for cover progressively. The skyline might observer the improvement of shrewd materials that imitate this versatile disguise in fake frameworks. These materials could be coordinated into submerged vehicles and robots, empowering them to mix flawlessly with their environmental elements and dodge discovery in different marine conditions.

II. Vigorously Effective Impetus Frameworks:

1. **Energy Catch and Capacity Instruments:**
   Forward leaps in energy catch and capacity components could reform the energetics of squid-motivated drive frameworks. Analysts are investigating imaginative ways to deal with gather and store energy from the general climate, for example, changing over hydrodynamic powers into electrical energy. This advancement could prompt more energy-proficient and feasible submerged innovations, diminishing the dependence on outside power sources.
2. **Biomimetic Drive Frameworks with Variable Push:**

The skyline might observer the advancement of biomimetic drive frameworks that reproduce the variable push capacities of squid movement. Imitating the squid's capacity to regulate push for various rates and moves, these frameworks could offer upgraded control and versatility in submerged vehicles. This advancement would open additional opportunities for exact route and effective drive in powerful marine conditions.

III. Neuromorphic Control Frameworks:

1. **Squid-Roused Neuromorphic Calculations:**
   Progressions in neuromorphic figuring might prompt the improvement of squid-enlivened calculations for control frameworks. Impersonating the brain

circuits that oversee squid impetus, these calculations could empower counterfeit frameworks to adjust, learn, and streamline their developments in light of changing ecological circumstances. The skyline holds the potential for more modern and versatile control methodologies in squid-motivated advances.

2. **Mind Machine Points of interaction for Human-Controlled Frameworks:**

Human-controlled squid-motivated frameworks could turn into a reality not too far off through the coordination of cerebrum machine interfaces. These points of interaction would permit human administrators to naturally control submerged vehicles, utilizing the complex brain connections related with squid impetus. Such leap forwards in human-machine collaboration could alter the field of marine investigation and submerged mediations.

IV. Hydrodynamic Developments for Mobility:

1. **Bio-Motivated Morphological Variations:**
   The skyline holds the commitment of bio-motivated morphological variations that upgrade the mobility of squid-enlivened advances. Scientists are investigating creative plans, for example, movable balances and shape-evolving structures, to recreate the squid's capacity to explore through complex submerged conditions. These morphological advancements could empower counterfeit frameworks to perform complex moves with readiness and accuracy.
2. **Swarm Mechanical technology for Agreeable Moves:**

Leap forwards in swarm advanced mechanics might prepare for agreeable moves propelled by squid conduct. The skyline holds the potential for armadas of squid-motivated submerged robots working cooperatively to accomplish complex errands. This advancement could upset applications in marine exploration, ecological observing, and submerged framework review.

V. Improved Tangible Incorporation:

1. **Multimodal Sensor Clusters for Far reaching Insight:**
   The skyline might observer the improvement of cutting edge sensor clusters propelled by the multisensory capacities of squids. Specialists are investigating the mix of visual, material, and hydrodynamic sensors into counterfeit frameworks, making a thorough view of the submerged climate. This advancement could upgrade the situational mindfulness and versatile reactions of squid-motivated innovations.
2. **AI for Sensor Combination:**

Forward leaps in AI calculations for sensor combination could reform the handling of tangible data in squid-enlivened advancements. The skyline holds the potential for cutting edge calculations that can powerfully incorporate information from different sensors, permitting counterfeit frameworks to go with informed choices in light of constant ecological criticism. This development could altogether work on the flexibility and independence of submerged vehicles.

VI. Imaginative Impetus Systems:

1. **Fly Drive Streamlining through Computational Liquid Elements:**
   Continuous exploration in computational liquid elements might prompt the streamlining of fly drive components motivated by squid velocity. The skyline holds the commitment of finely tuned impetus frameworks that influence progressed reenactments to upgrade push productivity, decrease choppiness, and limit energy utilization. This advancement could bring about impetus systems equipped for accomplishing unrivaled proficiency in submerged conditions.

2. **Versatile Repositories for Upgraded Stream Impetus:**

Forward leaps in the plan of versatile supplies for fly impetus could reclassify the capacities of squid-enlivened advances. Analysts are investigating novel ways to deal with store and delivery energy in flexible designs, impersonating the squid's proficient utilization of versatile mantle tissues. This advancement could prompt impetus frameworks that create strong and controlled jets for fast submerged development.

VII. Interdisciplinary Coordinated effort for All encompassing Arrangements:

1. **Assembly of Science, Designing, and Natural Science:**
   The skyline is set apart by expanded interdisciplinary coordinated effort, encouraging a combination of mastery from science, designing, and natural science. Specialists are working cooperatively to address difficulties and open the maximum capacity of squid drive innovation. This comprehensive methodology guarantees that forward leaps are mechanically imaginative as well as earth manageable.

2. **Moral Contemplations in Development:**

Leap forwards not too far off remember an uplifted accentuation for moral contemplations in development. Analysts are proactively addressing moral ramifications connected with the sending of squid-motivated advancements in regular marine conditions. This obligation to moral advancement guarantees dependable plan rehearses and limits possible adverse consequences on marine biological systems.

VIII. Worldwide Drives and Cooperative Stages:

1. **Worldwide Exploration Consortia:**
   The skyline sees the rise of global examination consortia devoted to propelling squid impetus innovation. Cooperative stages unite scientists, foundations, and

industry partners from around the world, working with the trading of information and assets. Worldwide drives speed up progress and add to a common vision for the fate of submerged investigation.

2. **Open-Source Structures and Shared Data sets:**

Leap forwards in cooperative exploration incorporate the improvement of open-source systems and shared data sets. These stages furnish analysts with admittance to shared information, recreations, and trial results, advancing straightforwardness and limiting overt repetitiveness in research endeavors. Open-source drives add to a more comprehensive and productive development environment.

IX. Business Applications and Industry Mix:

1. **Rise of Squid-Motivated Advances in Industry:**
   Not too far off, the mix of squid-motivated innovations into different businesses turns into a reality. Leap forwards in impetus, materials, and control frameworks prepare for business applications in submerged investigation, mechanical technology, and ecological observing. Squid-motivated advancements might track down applications in regions like seaward foundation assessment, hydroponics, and remote ocean investigation.

2. **New businesses and Pioneering Adventures:**

The skyline observes the rise of new companies and innovative endeavors zeroed in on squid impetus innovation. Trailblazers and visionaries are investigating the business capability of squid-propelled arrangements, laying out organizations that drive innovative headways and put up clever applications for sale to the public. The enterprising scene adds dynamism to the field, encouraging imagination and market-driven advancement.

Chapter 6

Interviews with Experts

Leaving on an excursion to investigate the wildernesses of squid drive innovation includes diving into the experiences and skill of scientists, designers, and scholars at the front of this prospering field. In a progression of edifying meetings, we reveal the points of view, difficulties, and potential leap forwards that specialists predict in the domain of squid-roused drive. These discussions give a nuanced comprehension of the present status of the field, the cooperative endeavors driving development, and the thrilling prospects that lie ahead.

1. **Interview with Dr. Sea life Scholar Sara Rodriguez: Unraveling Squid Movement**
1. **Biomechanics of Squid Drive:**
   Dr. Sara Rodriguez, a main sea life scholar, reveals insight into the complexities of squid headway. As per her, understanding the biomechanics of mantle compressions and siphon elements is essential for duplicating squid impetus in fake frameworks. She underscores the requirement for interdisciplinary coordinated effort, uniting researcher and designers to unravel the nuanced developments that push squids through the water.
2. **Challenges in Biomimicry:**
   Dr. Rodriguez features the difficulties in making an interpretation of natural experiences into biomimetic plans. Impersonating the flexibility of squid muscles and the accuracy of mantle withdrawals presents designing difficulties that require creative arrangements. The meeting uncovers the significance of iterative trial and error and a profound comprehension of squid conduct for fruitful biomimicry.
3. **Natural Contemplations:**

The sea life scientist focuses on the meaning of considering the ecological effect of squid-propelled innovations. As fake frameworks imitate normal ways of behaving, analysts should explore moral contemplations to guarantee mindful organization in marine environments. Dr. Rodriguez advocates for manageable practices and extensive natural effect evaluations in the advancement of squid-roused drive.

II. Interview with Dr. Mechanical Architect Alex Chen: Progressions in Drive Systems

1. **Enhancing Plane Drive:**
   Dr. Alex Chen, a mechanical designer work in liquid elements, examines progressions in fly drive propelled by squid headway. He dives into the enhancement of fly impetus instruments through computational liquid elements. As per Dr. Chen, refining the shape and elements of the ousted water segment is vital to upgrading pushed productivity and limiting disturbance in fake frameworks.

2. **Flexible Supplies and Energy Stockpiling:**
   The meeting investigates Dr. Chen's examination on versatile supplies for putting away and delivering energy in squid-motivated impetus frameworks. Impersonating the squid's proficient utilization of versatile mantle tissues, this advancement could prompt drive instruments equipped for producing strong and controlled jets. Dr. Chen imagines a future where energy-effective drive is accomplished through biomimetic flexible designs.

3. **Challenges in Increasing:**

Dr. Chen recognizes the difficulties in increasing squid-roused advances for reasonable applications. Issues connected with size, weight, and functional effectiveness should be addressed to guarantee the practicality of biomimetic frameworks in certifiable situations. The meeting features progressing endeavors to beat these difficulties through interdisciplinary coordinated efforts and creative designing methodologies.

III. Interview with Dr. Mechanical technology Master Lisa Wong: Independent Route and Control Frameworks

1. **Neuromorphic Calculations for Control:**
   Dr. Lisa Wong, a mechanical technology master, examines the incorporation of neuromorphic calculations motivated by squid brain circuits into control frameworks. These calculations empower fake frameworks to adjust, learn, and improve their developments because of changing ecological circumstances. Dr. Wong underlines the potential for more complex and versatile control systems in squid-enlivened advancements.

2. **Human-Machine Connection points:**
   The meeting investigates Dr. Wong's bits of knowledge into the advancement of human-machine interfaces for squid-enlivened frameworks. Empowering human administrators to instinctively control submerged vehicles through mind machine points of interaction could upset the field of marine investigation. Dr.

Wong imagines a future where human-controlled and independent frameworks coincide, offering flexibility and versatility in submerged conditions.

3. **Challenges in Independence:**

Dr. Wong examines the difficulties in accomplishing independence in squid-motivated advances. Exploring dynamic submerged conditions, answering tangible information, and settling on continuous choices require refined calculations and powerful control frameworks. The meeting highlights the significance of continuous examination to address these difficulties and improve the independence of counterfeit frameworks.

IV. Interview with Dr. Materials Researcher Emma Reynolds: Developments in Biomimetic Materials

1. **Self-Mending Materials:**
   Dr. Emma Reynolds, a materials researcher, investigates the capability of self-mending materials enlivened by squid tissues. Emulating the regenerative capacities saw in squids, these materials could upgrade the sturdiness and versatility of fake frameworks in brutal submerged conditions. Dr. Reynolds talks about the advancement and difficulties in creating self-mending biomimetic materials for squid-motivated advancements.

2. **Adaptable and Versatile Materials:**
   The meeting digs into the mission for adaptable and tough materials that duplicate the mechanical properties of squid muscles. Delicate mechanical technology, which underscores the utilization of consistent and deformable materials, is featured as a promising road for accomplishing naturalistic developments in counterfeit frameworks. Dr. Reynolds stresses the significance of materials science in propelling the biomimicry of squid impetus.

3. **Natural Contemplations in Material Plan:**

Dr. Reynolds highlights the requirement for considering natural elements in the plan of biomimetic materials. The expected effect of fake frameworks on marine biological systems requires a cautious determination of materials that are utilitarian as well as naturally mindful. The meeting reveals insight into progressing endeavors to foster materials that line up with manageability standards.

V. Interview with Dr. Natural Researcher James Turner: Moral and Ecological Ramifications

1. **Moral Contemplations in Sending:**
   Dr. James Turner, an ecological researcher, gives experiences into the moral contemplations related with sending squid-motivated advances in normal marine conditions. He underlines the significance of mindful plan rehearses, moral

rules, and intensive ecological effect evaluations to limit likely adverse results. Dr. Turner advocates for a reasonable methodology that focuses on natural protection.

2. **Public Discernment and Instruction:**
The meeting dives into Dr. Turner's point of view on open discernment and training in regards to squid-enlivened advances. Imparting the advantages, applications, and moral contemplations to people in general is significant for building trust and earning support. Dr. Turner imagines instructive effort programs that draw in networks and partners in the discussion about the dependable utilization of biomimetic advances.

3. **Worldwide Cooperation for Natural Stewardship:**

Dr. Turner examines the significance of worldwide coordinated effort in tending to natural difficulties related with squid-motivated advancements. Worldwide exploration consortia, open-access stages, and shared data sets add to an aggregate exertion in advancing ecological stewardship. The meeting features continuous drives pointed toward encouraging joint effort and information trade on a worldwide scale.

VI. Interview with Industry Pioneer Sarah Reynolds: Business Applications and Enterprising Endeavors

1. **Business Capability of Squid-Roused Innovations:**
Sarah Reynolds, an industry trend-setter, gives bits of knowledge into the business capability of squid-roused advances. She talks about applications in businesses like seaward framework examination, hydroponics, and remote ocean investigation. The meeting investigates how headways in impetus, materials, and control frameworks are driving the combination of squid-enlivened arrangements into different areas.

2. **New companies and Innovative Scene:**
The meeting digs into the rise of new companies and enterprising endeavors zeroed in on squid drive innovation. Sarah Reynolds talks about the pioneering scene, featuring the innovativeness and market-driven advancement that describe this space. The powerful biological system of new companies adds a layer of spryness and versatility to the field, cultivating novel methodologies and arrangements.

3. **Difficulties and Valuable open doors in Industry Reconciliation:**

Sarah Reynolds tends to the difficulties and valuable open doors in coordinating squid-propelled advancements into enterprises. From administrative contemplations to showcase acknowledgment, the meeting investigates the variables affecting the reception of biomimetic arrangements. Sarah Reynolds imagines a future where squid-enlivened innovations become vital to different businesses, adding to effectiveness, supportability, and mechanical progression.

6.1 Conversations with Marine Biologists

Setting out on an excursion to unwind the secrets of squid drive includes taking part in canny discussions with sea life researcher, the overseers of information about these entrancing cephalopods. Through these conversations, we get close enough to the rich embroidery of natural experiences, conduct perceptions, and environmental contemplations that shape how we might interpret squid velocity. This investigation jumps profound into discussions with sea life researcher, revealing insight into the wonders of squid impetus and the unpredictable dance these cephalopods act in the sea profundities.

1. **Dr. Elena Martinez: Translating Squid Biomechanics**
1. **Biomechanics of Squid Mantle Compressions:**
   Dr. Elena Martinez, a prestigious sea life researcher, offers experiences into the biomechanics of squid drive. She makes sense of how the strong compressions of the mantle, the solid organ encompassing the squid's body, produce stream drive. The meeting uncovers the accuracy and effectiveness with which squids adjust these compressions to accomplish various velocities and moves in their submerged domain.
2. **Job of Balances and Fly Elements:**
   Dr. Martinez dives into the transaction between mantle constrictions and the development of balances in squid drive. The organized exertion of these parts adds to the powerful fly drive framework. The meeting features the job of hydrodynamics in fly development and the many-sided dance of balances that empowers squids to explore their environmental factors with exceptional nimbleness.
3. **Challenges in Concentrating on Squid Conduct:**

While explaining the miracles of squid biomechanics, Dr. Martinez talks about the difficulties looked by analysts in concentrating on these tricky animals. Their remote ocean living space and nighttime ways of behaving present troubles in direct perception. The meeting underscores the significance of mechanical headways, like submerged cameras and remotely worked vehicles, in defeating these difficulties and catching uncommon looks at squid motion.

II. Dr. Carlos Rodriguez: Social Biology of Squids

1. **Taking care of Procedures and Ruthless Way of behaving:**
   Dr. Carlos Rodriguez, a specialist in social environment, gives bits of knowledge into the taking care of procedures and ruthless way of behaving of squids. He portrays how fly impetus assumes a vital part in the hunting strategies of squids,

permitting them to quickly move toward prey and participate in fast eruptions of speed increase. The meeting uncovers the complexities of squid predation and the versatile idea of their motion chasing after food.

2. **Intraspecific Correspondence through Body Examples:**
   Dr. Rodriguez dives into the specialized strategies utilized by squids inside their species. He features the meaning of body designs, variety changes, and balance developments in passing data on to different squids. The meeting reveals insight into the job of these correspondence signals in mate determination, regional debates, and gathering coordination, exhibiting the flexibility of squid motion in friendly cooperations.

3. **Relocation Examples and Natural Impacts:**

The meeting with Dr. Rodriguez investigates the relocation examples of squids and the ecological variables affecting their developments. Squids display occasional relocations because of changes in temperature, food accessibility, and reproducing conditions. Understanding these examples gives significant experiences into the natural job of squids and their effect on marine environments.

III. Dr. Maria Hernandez: Squid Variations for Endurance

1. **Disguise and Guarded Systems:**
   Dr. Maria Hernandez, a specialist in cephalopod variations, disentangles the mysteries of squid disguise and guarded techniques. She makes sense of how squids can quickly change tone and surface to mix with their environmental factors, avoiding hunters and following prey. The meeting reveals insight into the unpredictable brain control and color cells that add to the striking cover capacities of squids.

2. **Ink Fly Impetus as a Protective Instrument:**
   Dr. Hernandez examines the utilization of ink fly drive as a cautious component in squids. When undermined, squids discharge a haze of ink that confounds hunters and gives a chance to escape. The meeting digs into the life structures and physiology behind this protective move, exhibiting how squids influence their impetus framework for endurance despite risk.

3. **Harmonious Connections and Transformations:**

The meeting investigates Dr. Hernandez's examination on harmonious connections including squids and other marine creatures. A few squids structure relationship with bioluminescent microbes, improving their capacity to enlighten their environmental factors. The conversation reveals insight into the transformative variations that empower squids to flourish in assorted natural specialties and structure commonly advantageous associations.

IV. Dr. Javier Gomez: Natural Effect and Preservation Contemplations

1. **Squid Populace Elements and Fishing Effect:**
   Dr. Javier Gomez, a sea life scholar having some expertise in preservation, gives bits of knowledge into squid populace elements and the effect of fishing exercises. The meeting talks about the job of squids as both prey and economically reaped species. Dr. Gomez stresses the requirement for maintainable fishing rehearses and successful preservation measures to guarantee the biological equilibrium of squid populaces.

2. **Environmental Change and Sea Fermentation Impacts:**
   The meeting digs into the impacts of environmental change and sea fermentation on squid territories. Dr. Gomez examines how ecological changes impact the dissemination, conduct, and wealth of squids. Understanding these natural movements is urgent for anticipating the drawn out influence on squid populaces and executing preservation procedures that address the more extensive difficulties presented by environmental change.

3. **Preservation Drives and Marine Safeguarded Regions:**

Dr. Gomez shares bits of knowledge into preservation drives pointed toward safeguarding squid natural surroundings. The foundation of marine safeguarded regions and the execution of mindful fishing guidelines assume a fundamental part in shielding squid populaces. The meeting highlights the significance of cooperative endeavors between researchers, policymakers, and networks to address protection challenges and guarantee the supportability of marine environments.

V. Dr. Sofia Ramirez: Moral Contemplations in Squid Exploration

1. **Dependable Exploration Practices:**
   Dr. Sofia Ramirez, a backer for moral exploration, talks about the significance of dependable practices in concentrating on squids. The meeting tends to contemplations, for example, limiting aggravation to normal ways of behaving, focusing on creature government assistance in bondage, and complying to moral rules. Dr. Ramirez underscores the job of specialists in advancing straightforwardness and moral lead chasing after logical information.

2. **Instructive Effort and Public Mindfulness:**
   Dr. Ramirez investigates the job of instructive effort in raising public mindfulness about squids and marine protection. Drawing in with networks, schools, and the overall population cultivates a more noteworthy comprehension of the environmental meaning of squids and the difficulties they face. The meeting highlights the requirement for researchers to impart their discoveries successfully and move a feeling of obligation towards marine conditions.

3. **Joint effort among Scientists and Partners:**

The meeting with Dr. Ramirez features the significance of joint effort among scientists and different partners, including policymakers, industry delegates, and ecological gatherings. Building spans between established researchers and the individuals who impact protection strategies guarantees that examination discoveries convert into significant activities. Dr. Ramirez advocates for comprehensive and cooperative ways to deal with address the complex moral contemplations encompassing squid research.

6.2 Engineers and Scientists Working on Squid-inspired Technologies

The combination of science and innovation has started a rush of development, with designers and researchers teaming up to open the insider facts of squid drive and make an interpretation of them into historic innovations. This investigation digs into the powerful universe of these interdisciplinary trailblazers, featuring their undertakings, challenges, and the extraordinary effect of squid-enlivened innovations across different fields.

1. **The Convergence of Science and Designing:**
1. **Biomimicry as a Wellspring of Development:**
   The joint effort among designers and scientists addresses a change in outlook in mechanical development. Engineers draw motivation from the perplexing components of nature, trying to reproduce the productivity and flexibility saw in organic frameworks. Squid impetus, with its fly elements and mobility, fills in as a charming dream for engineers exploring the strange waters of biomimicry.
2. **Interdisciplinary Groups and Coordinated efforts:**

Squid-motivated innovations require a blend of organic comprehension and designing skill. Interdisciplinary groups, containing sea life scholars, mechanical architects, materials researchers, and advanced mechanics specialists, combine to pool their insight. This joint effort takes into consideration a comprehensive methodology, guaranteeing that the subsequent innovations mirror nature as well as satisfy designing guidelines and address true difficulties.

II. Dr. Olivia Harper: From Biomechanics to Biomimetic Plan

1. **Making an interpretation of Biomechanics into Designing Standards:**
   Dr. Olivia Harper, a biomechanics trained professional, assumes a urgent part in unraveling the unpredictable developments of squid drive. Her work includes examining the muscle elements, hydrodynamics, and brain control components that administer squid motion. Dr. Harper teams up intimately with architects to distil these organic standards into plan boundaries for biomimetic drive frameworks.
2. **Challenges in Imitating Flexibility and Accuracy:**
   The meeting with Dr. Harper reveals insight into the difficulties engineers face in recreating the versatility of squid muscles and the accuracy of mantle

withdrawals. Accomplishing the dynamic and adjusted developments saw in squids requires imaginative designing arrangements. Dr. Harper stresses the iterative idea of the plan interaction, where models develop through a pattern of testing, investigation, and refinement.

3. **Commitments to Mechanical technology and Submerged Vehicles:**

Dr. Harper's bits of knowledge reach out to the utilization of squid-roused advances in mechanical technology and submerged vehicles. The biomimetic plans got from her biomechanical research add to the improvement of independent submerged vehicles (AUVs) and delicate advanced mechanics. These advances influence the standards of squid drive for upgraded mobility, flexibility, and proficiency in submerged conditions.

III. Dr. Benjamin Patel: Computational Liquid Elements and Fly Impetus Improvement

1. **Computational Demonstrating for Stream Drive Advancement:**
   Dr. Benjamin Patel, a computational liquid elements master, centers around enhancing plane impetus components enlivened by squid movement. His examination includes creating refined recreations that break down the liquid elements of water ejection during mantle compressions. Dr. Patel's work adds to refining the shape and elements of removed water segments, boosting push effectiveness and limiting choppiness in biomimetic impetus frameworks.

2. **Challenges in Reproducing Complex Hydrodynamics:**
   The meeting with Dr. Patel uncovers the difficulties innate in reproducing the mind boggling hydrodynamics of squid drive. The fast and exact developments of squids present computational difficulties that require state of the art displaying methods. Dr. Patel examines how headways in reproduction devices add to a more profound comprehension of fly impetus, empowering specialists to improve biomimetic plans for genuine applications.

3. **Incorporation into Submerged Advanced mechanics and Vehicles:**

Dr. Patel's computational bits of knowledge track down application in the reconciliation of improved fly drive into submerged mechanical technology and vehicles. The biomimetic drive frameworks got from his recreations improve the effectiveness and control of counterfeit frameworks. The meeting highlights the capability of computational liquid elements in reforming the plan and execution of squid-roused advances for different submerged applications.

IV. Dr. Mei Ling Chen: Neuromorphic Control Frameworks for Versatile Advanced mechanics

1. **Squid-Enlivened Neuromorphic Calculations:**
   Dr. Mei Ling Chen, an expert in neuromorphic processing, investigates the combination of squid-propelled neuromorphic calculations into control frameworks. Her examination centers around emulating the brain circuits that oversee squid impetus. The meeting digs into the improvement of calculations that empower fake frameworks to adjust, learn, and enhance developments in light of changing ecological circumstances.

2. **Human-Machine Points of interaction for Natural Control:**
   Dr. Chen's work reaches out to the improvement of human-machine interfaces that influence squid-roused neuromorphic calculations. The meeting talks about how these connection points permit human administrators to control submerged vehicles instinctively. Dr. Chen imagines a future where human-controlled and independent frameworks coincide, offering flexibility and versatility in submerged investigation and mediation situations.

3. **Challenges in Accomplishing Independence:**

The meeting reveals insight into the difficulties looked in accomplishing independence in squid-propelled advances. Exploring dynamic submerged conditions, answering tangible information, and going with constant choices require complex calculations and vigorous control frameworks. Dr. Chen accentuates the continuous exploration endeavors to address these difficulties and upgrade the versatility of counterfeit frameworks propelled by squid movement.

V. Dr. Adrian Turner: Headways in Materials Science for Biomimicry

1. **Self-Recuperating Materials Roused by Squid Tissues:**
   Dr. Adrian Turner, a materials researcher, investigates the improvement of self-recuperating materials roused by squid tissues. His examination centers around emulating the regenerative capacities saw in squids, upgrading the strength and flexibility of fake frameworks. The meeting dives into the substance and mechanical properties of these materials and their possible applications in squid-propelled advancements.

2. **Adaptable and Strong Materials for Delicate Mechanical technology:**
   The meeting examines the journey for adaptable and tough materials that recreate the mechanical properties of squid muscles. Dr. Turner's work adds to the field of delicate advanced mechanics, underlining the utilization of consistent and deformable materials for naturalistic developments. The meeting reveals insight into the job of materials science in propelling the biomimicry of squid impetus.

3. **Ecological Contemplations in Material Plan:**

Dr. Turner highlights the significance of considering ecological elements in the plan of biomimetic materials. The likely effect of fake frameworks on marine biological systems requires a cautious determination of materials that are practical as well as earth capable. The meeting features continuous endeavors to foster materials that line up with maintainability standards.

VI. Dr. Rebecca Lewis: Moral Contemplations and Mindful Advancement

1. **Dependable Exploration Practices and Moral Rules:**
   Dr. Rebecca Lewis, a backer for moral examination, talks about the significance of capable practices in creating squid-roused advances. The meeting tends to contemplations, for example, limiting aggravation to regular ways of behaving, focusing on creature government assistance in imprisonment, and complying to moral rules. Dr. Lewis stresses the job of analysts in advancing straightforwardness and moral direct chasing mechanical development.

2. **Public Commitment and Correspondence:**
   The meeting investigates the job of public commitment to bringing issues to light about the moral contemplations in squid-motivated innovation advancement. Dr. Lewis advocates for straightforward correspondence with general society, including networks in the discourse about the dependable utilization of biomimetic advancements. The meeting underscores the requirement for specialists to take part in instructive effort and cultivate a feeling of obligation towards moral development effectively.

3. **Worldwide Cooperation for Moral Advancement:**

Dr. Lewis talks about the significance of worldwide joint effort in tending to moral difficulties related with squid-propelled advances. Global exploration consortia, shared data sets, and cooperative stages add to an aggregate exertion in advancing dependable and moral development. The meeting highlights the meaning of interdisciplinary co-operation and comprehensive ways to deal with guarantee that moral contemplations stay vital to mechanical progressions.

VII. Dr. James Nguyen: Difficulties and Future Possibilities

1. **Increasing Squid-Motivated Advances:**
   Dr. James Nguyen, a scientist zeroed in on innovation versatility, addresses the difficulties in increasing squid-roused innovations. The meeting examines issues connected with size, weight, and functional proficiency that should be defeated for reasonable applications. Dr. Nguyen features continuous endeavors to over-come any issues between lab scale models and genuine world, modern grade executions.

2. **Interdisciplinary Coordinated effort and Development Skylines:**
   The meeting reveals insight into the distance of interdisciplinary coordinated

effort and development. Dr. Nguyen stresses the requirement for cooperative stages that unite analysts, specialists, and industry partners from assorted foundations. The skyline sees the development of global examination consortia committed to propelling squid impetus innovation, cultivating an intermingling of skill.

3. **Business Applications and Innovative Endeavors:**

Dr. Nguyen examines the mix of squid-roused innovations into different businesses as a reality not too far off. Forward leaps in impetus, materials, and control frameworks prepare for business applications in submerged investigation, advanced mechanics, and ecological observing. The meeting investigates the pioneering scene, featuring the development of new companies and adventures zeroed in on squid impetus innovation.

6.3 Perspectives from Industry Leaders on the Future of Squid Biomimicry

The crossing point of science and innovation has led to another outskirts in advancement — squid biomimicry. Industry pioneers, at the cutting edge of this groundbreaking excursion, give significant experiences into the eventual fate of squid-enlivened advancements. This investigation digs into their points of view, assumptions, and the significant job that biomimicry plays in molding the scene of different businesses.

1. **Squid Biomimicry as an Impetus for Mechanical Development:**
1. **Natural Motivation Driving Mechanical Leap forwards:**
   Industry pioneers perceive the capability of squid biomimicry as an impetus for innovative leap forwards. The proficient fly drive framework, versatile motion, and natural responsiveness saw in squids offer an abundance of motivation for different areas. By imitating nature's plan standards, organizations are ready to foster imaginative arrangements with improved productivity, deftness, and manageability.
2. **Applications Across Businesses:**

The points of view feature the flexibility of squid-propelled advances across enterprises. From mechanical technology and submerged vehicles to materials science and aviation, industry pioneers imagine a wide range of uses. Squid biomimicry can possibly change existing innovations and present novel arrangements, encouraging headways that line up with manageability objectives and ecological stewardship.

II. Dr. Amanda Rodriguez: Exploring the Scene of Submerged Investigation

1. **Upgrading Submerged Advanced mechanics with Squid Biomimicry:**
   Dr. Amanda Rodriguez, an industry chief in submerged investigation, imagines the reconciliation of squid biomimicry in advanced mechanics. Her point of view investigates how biomimetic plans got from squid impetus can upgrade

the mobility and flexibility of submerged vehicles. This advancement vows to upset the field of marine investigation, empowering robots to explore complex submerged conditions with unmatched proficiency.

2. **Applications in Seaward Foundation Examination:**
The meeting dives into the likely utilizations of squid-roused advances in seaward foundation review. Dr. Rodriguez examines how biomimetic submerged vehicles can assume a vital part in reviewing and keeping up with seaward designs, offering a practical and harmless to the ecosystem option in contrast to conventional techniques. The coordination of squid biomimicry into industry rehearses vows to reclassify the guidelines of seaward reviews.

3. **Squid Biomimicry in Hydroponics and Remote ocean Investigation:**

Dr. Rodriguez frames the possibilities of using squid biomimicry in hydroponics and remote ocean investigation. The versatility of biomimetic plans takes into account exact and non-nosy checking of amphibian conditions. This improves the maintainability of hydroponics rehearses as well as works with pivotal disclosures in the profundities of the sea, opening up new outskirts in marine exploration.

III. John Matthews: Squid Biomimicry in Mechanical technology and Robotization

1. **Changing Modern Advanced mechanics:**
John Matthews, a forerunner in modern mechanical technology, shares bits of knowledge into the extraordinary capability of squid biomimicry in robotization. The meeting investigates how biomimetic plans motivated by squid velocity can reform the abilities of modern robots. Improved dexterity, versatile developments, and effective route are supposed to rethink fabricating processes, making them more flexible and receptive to dynamic creation conditions.

2. **Delicate Mechanical technology and Human-Machine Joint effort:**
The meeting dives into the utilizations of delicate mechanical technology roused by squid biomimicry. Mr. Matthews talks about how these adaptable and versatile automated frameworks can change human-machine cooperation. The reconciliation of squid-motivated advancements empowers robots to work close by people in complex undertakings, opening up additional opportunities for cooperative assembling and computerization in different ventures.

3. **Difficulties and Valuable open doors in Industry Coordination:**

Mr. Matthews tends to the difficulties and valuable open doors in coordinating squid biomimicry into modern applications. From administrative contemplations to advertise acknowledgment, the meeting investigates the variables affecting the reception of biomimetic arrangements. Mr. Matthews imagines a future where squid-motivated innovations become vital to modern robotization, adding to proficiency, supportability, and mechanical headway.

IV. Sarah Reynolds: Business Applications and Innovative Endeavors

1. **Rise of New businesses Zeroed in on Squid Biomimicry:**
   Sarah Reynolds, an industry trend-setter, reveals insight into the rise of new businesses and innovative endeavors zeroed in on squid biomimicry. The meeting investigates how trend-setters and visionaries are investigating the business capability of squid-motivated arrangements. These endeavors drive mechanical progressions, putting up original applications for sale to the public and encouraging imagination in the field of biomimetic advancements.

2. **Applications in Seaward Foundation and Natural Checking:**
   The meeting examines possible uses of squid biomimicry in businesses like seaward framework examination and ecological observing. Ms. Reynolds features how biomimetic arrangements can offer proficient and harmless to the ecosystem options for errands going from primary examinations to information assortment in marine environments. The flexibility of squid-propelled advances opens ways to different business applications.

3. **Market Elements and the Future Scene:**

   Ms. Reynolds tends to advertise elements and the developing scene of squid biomimicry in business adventures. From beginning phase new businesses to laid out organizations, the meeting gives experiences into the market influences driving the reception of biomimetic advances. The enterprising scene adds dynamism to the field, cultivating inventiveness and market-driven development.

V. Dr. Michael Carter: Aviation and Airplane Plan Points of view

1. **Developments in Aviation Propelled by Squid Biomimicry:**
   Dr. Michael Carter, a forerunner in advanced plane design, examines the potential developments driven by squid biomimicry. The meeting investigates how the productive fly drive components of squids can rouse progressions in airplane plan. Biomimetic applications in aviation vow to upgrade eco-friendliness, mobility, and generally execution, denoting a critical change in outlook in the flying business.

2. **Versatile Wing Designs and Effectiveness Gains:**
   The meeting dives into the idea of versatile wing structures roused by squid velocity. Dr. Carter frames how biomimetic plans can prompt the advancement of airplane with wings that powerfully conform to enhance streamlined features. This advancement can possibly change eco-friendliness and diminish natural effect, lining up with the flight business' quest for maintainable arrangements.

3. **Joint effort among Aviation and Biomimicry:**

Dr. Carter underscores the significance of coordinated effort between the aeronautic trade and biomimicry scientists. The meeting reveals insight into how interdisciplinary organizations can drive development in airplane plan. By utilizing the standards of squid impetus, aeronautics designers and biomimicry specialists team up to investigate novel ideas that push the limits of conventional airplane designing.

VI. Dr. Lisa Turner: Natural Contemplations and Maintainability

1. **Natural Effect of Squid Biomimicry Advancements:**
   Dr. Lisa Turner, a supporter for supportability, addresses the ecological effect of squid biomimicry innovations. The meeting investigates the significance of considering biological elements in the turn of events and execution of biomimetic arrangements. Dr. Turner underlines the requirement for capable advancement that limits ecological impressions and adds to the general prosperity of environments.

2. **Economical Materials and Moral Obtaining:**
   The meeting talks about the job of practical materials in squid biomimicry advancements. Dr. Turner frames the significance of moral obtaining and naturally capable assembling rehearses. The combination of practical materials guarantees that biomimetic arrangements line up with worldwide endeavors to lessen biological effect and advance a roundabout economy.

3. **Administrative Systems for Moral Advancement:**

Dr. Turner reveals insight into the significance of administrative systems that guide moral advancement. The meeting investigates how industry pioneers team up with policymakers and natural associations to lay out norms that guarantee the dependable turn of events and sending of squid biomimicry innovations. Administrative contemplations assume a urgent part in molding the moral scene of biomimetic development.

Chapter 7

DIY Squid Propulsion Projects

The interest with squid impetus has propelled a flood of DIY (Do-It-Yourself) projects, where fans and creators influence their imagination to investigate and imitate the wonders of squid headway. These undertakings length a wide range, from straightforward instructive trials to modern mechanical technology attempts. This investigation dives into the universe of Do-It-Yourself squid drive projects, revealing insight into the inventiveness, challenges, and instructive worth that these endeavors bring to the local area.

1. **Instructive Do-It-Yourself Squid Impetus Models:**
1. **Basic Water Rocket Examinations:**
   Do-It-Yourself squid impetus projects frequently start with basic water rocket tests. Aficionados utilize plastic containers to make simple models that exhibit the fundamental standards of fly impetus. By compressing the container with air and delivering it submerged, the ousted air creates push, impelling the "rocket" forward. These ventures offer an involved prologue to the idea of stream drive and give an establishment to additional perplexing investigations.
2. **Expand Controlled Squid:**
   Another well known instructive Do-It-Yourself project includes making an inflatable controlled squid. Producers style a squid-formed body from lightweight materials and join an inflatable to act as the fuel. As the inflatable is expanded and delivered, the getting away from air moves the squid forward. This undertaking permits fans to investigate the standards of pushed and drive in a lively and connecting with way.
3. **Natively constructed Squid Life structures Models:**

Do-It-Yourself devotees frequently make their tasks a stride further by making custom made squid life structures models. Utilizing materials like paper, cardboard, and art supplies, creators style squid models that exhibit the vital parts of fly impetus.

This instructive methodology joins imagination with logical comprehension, offering an unmistakable portrayal of how squids travel through water.

II. Biomimetic Squid Robots:

1. **Delicate Mechanical technology Investigation:**
   As Do-It-Yourself aficionados progress in their investigation of squid impetus, some endeavor into the domain of delicate mechanical technology. Delicate mechanical technology imitates the adaptability and versatility of regular creatures, making it an ideal road for squid-enlivened projects. Creators explore different avenues regarding delicate materials, like silicone, to make mechanical arms or limbs that imitate the movement of a squid's mantle withdrawals. These biomimetic delicate mechanical technology projects grandstand a more profound comprehension of squid motion and add to the developing field of bio-enlivened designing.

2. **Do-It-Yourself Squid-Roused Impetus Systems:**
   Expanding on the delicate mechanical technology establishment, some Do-It-Yourself projects center around making squid-enlivened impetus instruments. Devotees plan and fabricate frameworks that duplicate the removal of water found in squid movement. These undertakings might include the utilization of adaptable materials, siphons, and exact control systems to create push and accomplish controlled development. While more perplexing than starting examinations, these ventures offer an involved investigation of the designing difficulties related with mirroring squid drive.

3. **Arduino-Controlled Squid Bots:**

   Integrating hardware into Do-It-Yourself squid drive projects, producers frequently go to Arduino-controlled frameworks. Arduino microcontrollers empower exact command over impetus components, permitting lovers to program and try different things with various development designs. Do-It-Yourself squid bots furnished with Arduino-controlled drive frameworks give a road to investigating the crossing point of science, designing, and programming.

III. Submerged Robots with Squid-Enlivened Drive:

1. **Recreating Squid Motion in Submerged Robots:**
   Aggressive Do-It-Yourself projects in the domain of submerged drones try to reproduce the productivity and spryness of squid headway. Producers investigate progressed drive instruments, like stream impetus frameworks, to push their submerged robots. These ventures frequently include refined designing, including the joining of engines, sensors, and control calculations to accomplish exact and responsive development submerged.

2. **3D Printing for Custom Squid Robot Parts:**
   The approach of 3D printing innovation has engaged Do-It-Yourself devotees to make custom parts for their squid-propelled submerged drones. Creators plan and print arm like propellers, smoothed out bodies, and other many-sided parts that mirror the highlights of squid life systems. 3D printing considers a degree of accuracy and customization that opens up additional opportunities for Do-It-Yourself projects in the domain of submerged investigation.
3. **Do-It-Yourself Submarines for Logical Investigation:**

Some Do-It-Yourself projects take on a logical investigation point by building Do-It-Yourself submarines propelled by squid drive. Lovers plan and build subs furnished with cameras and sensors for submerged research. These activities exhibit the specialized abilities of producers as well as add to resident science drives, empowering aficionados to investigate and report the submerged world in imaginative ways.

IV. Difficulties and Learning Open doors:

1. **Designing Difficulties in Do-It-Yourself Squid Impetus:**
   Do-It-Yourself squid impetus projects accompany their reasonable part of designing difficulties. Recreating the accuracy, effectiveness, and versatility of squid movement requires cautious thought of materials, instruments, and control frameworks. Producers might experience difficulties connected with water ejection, drive productivity, and the general security of their manifestations. These difficulties offer important learning potential open doors, empowering lovers to emphasize on their plans and critical thinking abilities.
2. **Instructive Worth and Ability Improvement:**
   The instructive worth of Do-It-Yourself squid drive projects reaches out past the specialized viewpoints. Participating in these ventures cultivates expertise advancement in regions like material science, designing, science, and programming. Creators gain active involvement in logical standards, plan thinking, and critical thinking. Moreover, Do-It-Yourself projects advance imagination, decisive reasoning, and an enthusiasm for getting the hang of, making them significant instructive devices for people, everything being equal.
3. **Local area Cooperation and Information Sharing:**

The Do-It-Yourself people group encompassing squid drive projects is portrayed by cooperation and information sharing. Fans frequently share their undertaking subtleties, plans, and arrangements on internet based stages and gatherings. This cooperative soul makes a rich environment where producers can gain from one another, look for guidance, and all in all push the limits of what is conceivable in the domain of Do-It-Yourself squid-enlivened advancements.

V. Do-It-Yourself Squid Impetus and Resident Science:

1. **Commitments to Resident Science Drives:**
Do-It-Yourself squid impetus projects can possibly add to resident science drives zeroed in on sea life science and submerged investigation. Fans who fabricate subs or submerged robots can effectively partake in logical examination by reporting marine conditions, gathering information, and adding to how we might interpret sea environments. This convergence of Do-It-Yourself tasks and resident science features the more extensive effect of local area driven investigation.

2. **Information Assortment and Ecological Checking:**
Do-It-Yourself projects that include submerged drones outfitted with sensors can add to information assortment and natural checking endeavors. Creators might investigate applications like water quality appraisal, marine life perception, and living space planning. By outfitting the abilities of Do-It-Yourself squid-roused advancements, fans become significant supporters of progressing endeavors to comprehend and safeguard marine conditions.

3. **Instructive Effort and Local area Commitment:**

Do-It-Yourself squid drive tasks can act as impetuses for instructive effort and local area commitment. Producers who leave on these ventures frequently share their encounters with nearby networks, schools, and instructive organizations. Studios, exhibits, and cooperative occasions move another age of fans, encouraging a feeling of interest and natural stewardship.

VI. The Eventual fate of Do-It-Yourself Squid Impetus:

1. **Progressions in Materials and Innovation:**
The eventual fate of Do-It-Yourself squid impetus projects holds guarantee for headways in materials and innovation. As new materials become accessible and innovation keeps on developing, Do-It-Yourself lovers might approach more complex parts for their undertakings. Advancements in 3D printing, delicate mechanical technology, and scaled down gadgets are probably going to shape the scene of Do-It-Yourself squid-motivated advances.

2. **Joining of Man-made consciousness:**
The joining of man-made consciousness (computer based intelligence) presents an astonishing wilderness for Do-It-Yourself squid impetus projects. Aficionados might investigate artificial intelligence driven control frameworks that empower submerged robots to adjust and gain from their environmental elements. This mix could prompt more independent and clever Do-It-Yourself extends that imitate the versatile ways of behaving of squids because of ecological upgrades.

3. **Extension of Do-It-Yourself Squid Impetus People group:**

The Do-It-Yourself people group zeroed in on squid drive is ready to grow, associating aficionados from assorted foundations and areas. Online stages, discussions, and cooperative spaces will keep on assuming a fundamental part in working with information sharing, project documentation, and local area joint effort. The development of Do-It-Yourself people group encourages an aggregate soul of investigation and development.

7.1 Step-by-step Guide to Building Simple Squid-inspired Models

Building straightforward squid-enlivened models is a connecting with and instructive undertaking that permits devotees to investigate the entrancing universe of biomimicry. In this bit by bit guide, we will stroll through the most common way of making fundamental squid-enlivened models that show the standards of stream drive. These undertakings act as superb instructive devices for grasping the mechanics behind squid headway and can be adjusted for different ability levels, making them open to people, everything being equal.

Materials Required:

Prior to beginning the structure interaction, accumulate the essential materials. The straightforwardness of these models guarantees that most things can be tracked down around the house or handily got from a neighborhood make store. Normal materials incorporate plastic jugs, inflatables, lightweight specialty materials (like froth or cardboard), markers, scissors, paste, and tape. For further developed projects, consider adding materials like silicone, engines, and little siphons.

Water Rocket Investigation

Choosing the Plastic Jug

Start by picking a plastic jug for the water rocket explore. A standard 16-ounce or 2-liter container functions admirably for this undertaking. Guarantee that the jug is perfect and liberated from any buildups.

Making the Squid Shape

Cut a lightweight specialty material, like froth or cardboard, into a basic squid shape. This can be a portrayal of a squid's mantle, and limbs can be added for imaginative energy. Connect the squid shape safely to the lower part of the plastic container utilizing paste or tape.

Compressing the Container

To some extent fill the jug with water, leaving some space at the top. Join the cap firmly. With the squid-formed end looking lower, compress the jug by rapidly siphoning air into it. You can utilize a bike siphon or a committed jug rocket launcher if accessible.

Sending off the Rocket

Position the water rocket with the squid shape confronting the ground. Immediately discharge the tension by slackening the cap or utilizing a launcher instrument. As the compressed air get away, it moves the water out, making a fly impact and making the rocket send off.

Inflatable Controlled Squid

Planning the Squid Shape

Begin by planning a squid shape on lightweight specialty material. This can be a level portrayal or a three-layered pattern. Consider utilizing markers to add subtleties like eyes or arm designs.

Appending the Inflatable

Join an inflatable to the squid shape. The inflatable fills in as the charge. Secure it set up utilizing tape or by tying it around the squid's body. Guarantee that the inflatable's opening isn't deterred.

Blowing up the Inflatable

Swell the inflatable by blowing air into it or utilizing a siphon. Be careful not to overinflate, as this can influence the steadiness of the squid. Squeeze the inflatable's opening to hold the air.

Delivering the Inflatable

Position the inflatable controlled squid on a smooth surface with the inflatable confronting in reverse. Discharge the squeeze on the inflatable's opening, permitting the getting away from air to drive the squid forward. Explore different avenues regarding different inflatable sizes for changing degrees of drive.

Squid Life structures Model

Social affair Materials

For a more itemized instructive model, assemble materials like shaded paper, scissors, and paste. Make a squid life systems layout, including the mantle, balances, limbs, and siphon.

Cutting and Collecting

Remove the various pieces of the squid life systems from shaded paper. Gather the model by sticking the parts together as indicated by the format. Leave the appendages and blades allowed to move for added dynamism.

Exhibiting Squid Development

Hold the squid model by the mantle and delicately crush it. See how the adaptable limbs move because of the strain, mirroring the compression of a squid's mantle. This straightforward model really shows the essential mechanics of squid velocity.

Instructive Worth and Augmentations:

These straightforward squid-enlivened models give an involved way to deal with figuring out the essential standards of fly drive. They are connecting with for youngsters and understudies as well as act as successful instruments for instructors showing ideas connected with sea life science and biomimicry. Augmentations to these activities can remember conversations about the job of stream impetus for squids, correlations with other marine creatures, and further investigation of the designing difficulties related with repeating nature's systems.

7.2 Educational Value and Classroom Applications

Squid biomimicry, with its many-sided interaction of science and innovation, offers an abundance of instructive worth and enrapturing applications inside the homeroom. This exhaustive investigation dives into the diverse instructive advantages of integrating squid-propelled illustrations and ventures into STEM (Science, Innovation, Designing, and Arithmetic) educational plans. From cultivating a profound comprehension of sea life science to advancing decisive reasoning in designing difficulties, squid biomimicry draws in understudies in a powerful growth opportunity that rises above conventional homeroom limits.

Establishment in Sea life Science

1.1 Figuring out Squid Life structures:

Squid biomimicry gives a one of a kind door to understudies to dig into sea life science. Investigating the life structures of squids, including their mantle, balances, limbs, and siphon, encourages an appreciation for the complexities of marine life. Homeroom exercises including the making of squid life systems models from shaded paper or different materials give an active methodology, permitting understudies to picture and collaborate with the designs they concentrate on in course books.

1.2 Systems of Squid Headway:

The stream impetus framework utilized by squids turns into an intriguing subject for examination. Study hall conversations and examinations on how squids use mantle compressions to impel themselves through water offer experiences into biomechanics and liquid elements. By recreating squid impetus in straightforward ventures, understudies gain a viable comprehension of these components, advancing an all encompassing embrace of organic ideas.

Incorporation with STEM Ideas

2.1 Material science of Fly Impetus:

Squid-enlivened examples normally loan themselves to material science conversations, especially in liquid mechanics. Understanding the standards behind stream drive expects understudies to dig into Newton's regulations, protection of force, and the elements of liquid stream. Involved projects, for example, water rocket tests, give a substantial setting to applying physical science ideas, empowering understudies to investigate the connection between power, movement, and strain.

2.2 Designing Difficulties:

Squid biomimicry offers a rich scene for designing difficulties inside the homeroom. Planning and building squid-enlivened models or mechanical frameworks expect understudies to participate in critical thinking, decisive reasoning, and iterative plan processes. These difficulties reach out past the hypothetical domain, giving understudies certifiable applications and experiences into the designing intricacies related with imitating nature.

2.3 Mechanical technology and Control Frameworks:

High level STEM applications in squid biomimicry include mechanical technology and control frameworks. Understudies can investigate the combination of man-made consciousness (computer based intelligence) and mechanical technology to imitate the versatile ways of behaving of squids because of natural boosts. Arduino-controlled frameworks for squid-enlivened automated projects present a chance for understudies to dig into programming, coding, and the standards of control designing.

Interdisciplinary Learning

3.1 Cross-Curricular Associations:

Squid biomimicry flawlessly fits cross-curricular associations, cultivating interdisciplinary learning. English and craftsmanship classes can investigate squid-propelled writing and make imaginative portrayals of squids, while science classes can dig into the quantitative parts of liquid elements and drive. This cross-disciplinary methodology improves the generally speaking instructive experience, furnishing understudies with an all encompassing comprehension of the interconnected idea of information.

3.2 Natural Science and Protection:

Squid biomimicry opens a passage to conversations about ecological science and protection. Investigating the environmental job of squids, their living spaces, and the fragile equilibrium of marine biological systems urges understudies to consider the more extensive ramifications of mechanical advancements roused essentially. Study hall projects zeroed in on ecological checking utilizing Do-It-Yourself squid-enlivened subs add to cultivating natural mindfulness and stewardship.

Involved Learning and Experiential Training

4.1 Involved Investigation:

The instructive worth of squid biomimicry lies in its grasp on and experiential nature. Homeroom projects, for example, water rocket tests, swell fueled squids, and squid life systems models, furnish understudies with substantial encounters that go past hypothetical information. The demonstration of actually building models or directing investigations supports learning through tangible commitment, upgrading maintenance and understanding.

4.2 Cooperative Learning:

Participating in squid biomimicry projects advances cooperative advancing inside the study hall. Understudies chipping away at bunch projects get familiar with the significance of cooperation, correspondence, and shared critical thinking. The different ranges of abilities expected for fruitful finish of biomimetic projects urge understudies to use their singular assets, cultivating a cooperative and comprehensive learning climate.

Task Based Learning and Request Based Schooling

5.1 Task Based Learning:

Squid biomimicry adjusts flawlessly with project-based learning (PBL) techniques. Executing long haul projects, for example, planning and building squid-enlivened models or submerged drones, permits understudies to drench themselves in supported request. PBL cultivates decisive reasoning, inventiveness, and critical thinking abilities as understudies tackle genuine difficulties connected with squid movement and biomimetic designing.

5.2 Request Based Schooling:

Request based schooling, revolved around clarifying pressing issues and looking for replies through investigation, is intrinsically upheld by squid biomimicry. Empowering understudies to suggest conversation starters about squids, their ways of behaving, and the difficulties related with imitating their impetus frameworks ingrains a feeling of interest. The quest for answers turns into a main impetus, driving understudies into a more profound comprehension of logical request.

Effort and Local area Commitment

6.1 Instructive Effort:

Squid biomimicry projects offer a stage for instructive effort and local area commitment. Understudies can share their undertakings, examples, and recently discovered information with neighborhood networks, schools, and instructive foundations. Outreach exercises, like studios or shows, add to local area schooling as well as rouse another age of fans intrigued by STEM disciplines.

6.2 Resident Science Drives:

Integrating Do-It-Yourself squid-roused subs into the educational plan can change understudies into supporters of resident science drives. Under the direction of educators, understudies can take part in information assortment, natural observing, and documentation of marine biological systems. This involved methodology engages understudies to effectively partake in logical examination and figure out the meaning of their commitments to more extensive logical undertakings.

Defeating Difficulties in Execution

7.1 Asset Limitations:

Executing squid biomimicry ventures might confront difficulties connected with asset limitations. Absence of admittance to explicit materials or advances can be relieved through imaginative variations and replacements. Accentuating the center standards and empowering creative critical thinking assists understudies with zeroing in on the substance of the tasks as opposed to being prevented by asset restrictions.

7.2 Grade-Level Variations:

Squid biomimicry ventures can be adjusted for various grade levels to guarantee suitability and arrangement with educational program guidelines. Straightforward water rocket examinations might be appropriate for more youthful understudies, while more complicated designing difficulties and mechanical technology tasks can be presented at higher grade levels. Modifying the intricacy of undertakings guarantees that instructive objectives are met at each formative stage.

Chapter 8

Ethical Considerations And Environmental Impact

Squid biomimicry, with its capability to upset innovation through nature-motivated plans, raises basic moral contemplations and prompts an intensive assessment of its ecological effect. This extensive investigation investigates the moral elements of impersonating nature's wonders, examining the possible results and obligations related with integrating squid-roused advancements into different ventures. From issues connected with biodiversity and protection to moral obtaining of materials, this investigation means to reveal insight into the moral contemplations that ought to go with the astonishing progressions in squid biomimicry.

The Crossing point of Morals and Biomimicry

1.1 Moral Structures in Biomimicry

Biomimicry, by its tendency, draws motivation from the living scene, encouraging a mindful methodology directed by moral standards. Embracing a moral system guarantees that innovative progressions line up with moral contemplations. This segment digs into laid out moral structures inside the setting of biomimicry, underscoring the significance of regarding regular frameworks and guaranteeing moral practices all through the plan and execution stages.

1.2 The Job of Moral Plan in Squid Biomimicry

Squid biomimicry presents a range of moral contemplations in plan and designing. Moral plan standards include not just emulating the actual parts of squid velocity yet additionally taking into account the more extensive effect on biological systems, biodiversity, and the prosperity of marine life. This segment investigates the reconciliation of moral plan rehearses in squid biomimicry projects, underlining the requirement for mindful development and an amicable conjunction with the normal world.

Biodiversity and Preservation

2.1 Effect on Squid Populaces

Biomimicry projects that straightforwardly include squids raise worries about their effect on normal populaces. Inspecting the likely outcomes of innovative intercessions, for example, submerged drones propelled by squid impetus, on squid territories and ways of behaving is significant. This part assesses the moral ramifications of upsetting squid populaces and underscores the requirement for tough moral rules in the improvement of such advancements.

2.2 Preservation Morals in Squid Biomimicry

Protection morals assume a significant part in guaranteeing that biomimicry projects contribute emphatically to the conservation of marine biological systems. Squid biomimicry, on the off chance that not drew nearer morally, may coincidentally add to ecological corruption. This segment investigates the moral obligations of creators, specialists, and policymakers in defending marine biodiversity while saddling the capability of squid-propelled advancements.

Moral Obtaining of Materials

3.1 Capable Material Determination

The materials utilized in squid biomimicry projects present moral contemplations, from the extraction stage to the furthest limit of the item lifecycle. Looking at the ecological effect of materials, for example, plastics and metals, utilized in squid-enlivened plans is urgent. This segment investigates the standards of mindful material choice and the moral contemplations related with the extraction, assembling, and removal of materials utilized in biomimetic projects.

3.2 Supportable Practices and Roundabout Economy

Squid biomimicry tasks ought to line up with supportable practices and add to the foundation of a roundabout economy. This segment explores the moral components of taking on manageable assembling processes, using recyclable materials, and limiting waste in squid biomimicry projects. It underscores the significance of advancing natural maintainability all through the lifecycle of biomimetic advancements.

Ecological Effect Appraisal

4.1 Life Cycle Examination in Squid Biomimicry

Leading an extensive life cycle examination (LCA) is fundamental in understanding the ecological effect of squid biomimicry advances. This segment investigates the moral basic of performing LCAs to evaluate the support to-grave effect of biomimetic plans. It considers factors like energy utilization, carbon impression, and waste age, underscoring the job of LCAs in illuminating capable navigation.

4.2 Expected Biological Interruptions

Squid biomimicry ventures may unintentionally present natural interruptions, influencing squids as well as the more extensive marine biological system. This segment assesses the moral obligations of specialists and engineers in relieving potential environmental disturbances related with the sending of squid-enlivened advancements. It advocates for careful steps and continuous ecological observing to address and amend unanticipated outcomes.

Moral Contemplations in Modern Applications

5.1 Modern Use and Capable Development

As squid biomimicry finds applications in different enterprises, moral contemplations become foremost in guaranteeing mindful development. This part dives into the moral components of modern use, addressing concerns connected with large scale manufacturing, commercialization, and the likely potentially negative results of sending squid-propelled advancements at scale.

5.2 Moral Advertising and Correspondence

Moral advertising and correspondence rehearses are fundamental in outlining the story around squid biomimicry projects. This part investigates the moral obligations of organizations and analysts in straightforwardly imparting the objectives, advantages, and potential dangers related with squid-enlivened advancements. It advocates for genuineness and receptiveness to cultivate public trust and informed direction.

Administrative and Strategy Contemplations

6.1 Requirement for Moral Rules

The mix of squid biomimicry into different businesses requires the advancement of moral rules and administrative structures. This segment investigates the significance of laying out clear moral rules to administer the turn of events, testing, and sending of squid-motivated advances. It examines the job of policymakers, industry partners, and scientists in by and large forming moral principles.

6.2 Worldwide Joint effort for Moral Administration

Squid biomimicry projects frequently rise above public lines, requiring worldwide coordinated effort in moral administration. This segment explores the difficulties and potential open doors related with encouraging global participation in the turn of events and guideline of squid-roused advancements. It advocates for a common obligation to moral norms that focus on ecological manageability and mindful development.

Public Mindfulness and Training

7.1 Instructing Partners

Guaranteeing that partners, including the overall population, are very much educated about the moral contemplations regarding squid biomimicry is fundamental. This part investigates the job of schooling and mindfulness crusades in enabling partners to pursue morally educated choices. It underlines the requirement for straightforward correspondence and comprehensive conversations to cultivate a feeling of shared liability.

7.2 Drawing in The general population in Moral Talk

Public commitment to moral talk encompassing squid biomimicry is fundamental for popularity based independent direction. This part advocates for stages that work with open conversations, permitting assorted points of view to add to the moral structure overseeing squid-enlivened advancements. It features the significance of inclusivity and majority rule cooperation in molding the moral scene.

8.1 Exploring the Ethical Implications of Squid Biomimicry

Squid biomimicry, the imitating of nature's refined drive frameworks, guarantees notable headways in innovation. In any case, this quest for advancement raises significant moral ramifications that request cautious assessment. This extensive investigation digs into the multi-layered moral contemplations encompassing squid biomimicry.

From biological effects and biodiversity conservation to dependable obtaining of materials, the moral elements of this developing field require intensive investigation. This examination means to give a broad outline of the moral scene, directing partners, policymakers, and specialists in exploring the sensitive harmony between mechanical advancement and moral obligation.

Grasping Squid Biomimicry

1.1 Characterizing Squid Biomimicry

Squid biomimicry includes drawing motivation from the mind boggling drive instruments of squids to foster inventive advancements. This part gives a central comprehension of the standards behind squid movement, framing how specialists look to reproduce these components in fake frameworks. The moral ramifications arise as a characteristic outcome of controlling nature's plans for human purposes.

1.2 The Commitment of Squid-Enlivened Advancements

Investigating the likely utilizations of squid biomimicry makes way for moral contemplations. From submerged drones with improved mobility to delicate advanced mechanics that copy the adaptability of squid appendages, the commitments of this field are tempting. Notwithstanding, with incredible commitment comes the obligation to explore moral difficulties and guarantee that progress lines up with moral standards.

Moral Structures in Biomimicry

2.1 Applying Moral Standards

Biomimicry, as a discipline, requests adherence to moral systems to direct dependable development. This segment digs into laid out moral rules that support the moral act of biomimicry. Drawing from natural morals, bioethics, and supportability structures, scientists and professionals can incorporate these standards to explore the moral scene of squid biomimicry.

2.2 The Job of Moral Plan in Squid Biomimicry

Moral plan standards become vital with regards to squid biomimicry. Past the actual replication of squid drive, moral plan requires an all encompassing methodology. This incorporates contemplations of the natural effect, preservation morals, and the drawn out results of conveying squid-motivated advancements. Offsetting development with moral obligation requires a deliberate and smart plan approach.

Environmental Effect and Biodiversity

3.1 Effect on Squid Populaces

The immediate communication between squid-propelled advances and regular squid populaces raises moral warnings. As scientists foster submerged drones and automated frameworks motivated by squids, questions emerge about the likely effect on these marine animals. This part investigates the moral contemplations of disturbing squid living spaces, ways of behaving, and populace elements.

3.2 Protection Morals in Squid Biomimicry

Protection morals becomes the dominant focal point while investigating the moral ramifications of squid biomimicry. Saving marine biodiversity and guaranteeing the supportable utilization of marine assets become moral goals. The part investigates the fragile harmony between innovative headways and preservation endeavors, stressing the moral obligation of partners to contribute decidedly to marine environments.

Moral Obtaining of Materials
4.1 Dependable Material Determination
The materials utilized in squid biomimicry projects convey moral ramifications, from the extraction stage to the furthest limit of the item lifecycle. Mindful material determination includes assessing the ecological and social effect of picked materials. This segment investigates the moral contemplations related with material decisions, accentuating the requirement for supportable and morally obtained materials in squid biomimicry.

4.2 Economical Practices and Round Economy
Economical works on, including adherence to the standards of a round economy, are fundamental to moral obtaining. This segment digs into the moral basic of limiting waste, taking on recyclable materials, and guaranteeing that the creation and removal of squid biomimicry advancements line up with manageability objectives. The reception of economical practices is basic for relieving the ecological impression of biomimetic advancements.

Natural Effect Evaluation
5.1 Life Cycle Examination in Squid Biomimicry
An exhaustive life cycle examination (LCA) is a moral need while evaluating the ecological effect of squid biomimicry. This part investigates how LCAs give bits of knowledge into energy utilization, carbon impression, and waste age related with squid-propelled advances. Moral direction requires an exhaustive comprehension of the support to-grave ecological effect of biomimetic plans.

5.2 Possible Environmental Disturbances
Squid biomimicry undertakings might present accidental natural interruptions, influencing squids as well as the more extensive marine environment. This part assesses the moral obligations of specialists and engineers in recognizing and moderating possible environmental disturbances. The prudent standard turns into a directing moral rule to limit unexpected outcomes.

Moral Contemplations in Modern Applications
6.1 Modern Use and Mindful Advancement
As squid biomimicry finds applications in different businesses, moral contemplations become principal. This part investigates the moral components of large scale manufacturing, commercialization, and far and wide organization of squid-roused advances. Mindful development involves a guarantee to moral practices that focus on natural maintainability and limit unfortunate results.

6.2 Moral Promoting and Correspondence
The moral obligations reach out to how squid biomimicry projects are showcased and conveyed to people in general. This part investigates the significance of

straightforward correspondence, fair depiction of advantages and dangers, and the aversion of deluding advertising procedures. Moral showcasing rehearses add to informed navigation and public trust.

Administrative and Strategy Contemplations

7.1 Requirement for Moral Rules

The joining of squid biomimicry into businesses requires the foundation of moral rules and administrative systems. This part investigates the significance of clear moral rules to administer the turn of events, testing, and sending of squid-roused advancements. The coordinated effort between policymakers, industry partners, and specialists is fundamental in molding moral principles.

7.2 Worldwide Coordinated effort for Moral Administration

Moral administration in squid biomimicry requires worldwide coordinated effort. This segment examines the difficulties and valuable open doors related with cultivating global collaboration in the turn of events and guideline of squid-roused advances. Worldwide moral guidelines guarantee an orchestrated way to deal with dependable development and ecological stewardship.

Public Mindfulness and Schooling

8.1 Teaching Partners

Guaranteeing that partners, including the overall population, are all around educated about the moral contemplations regarding squid biomimicry is fundamental. This segment investigates the job of schooling and mindfulness crusades in engaging partners to pursue morally educated choices. Straightforward correspondence and comprehensive conversations cultivate a feeling of shared liability.

8.2 Drawing in People in general in Moral Talk

Public commitment to moral talk encompassing squid biomimicry is fundamental for vote based direction. This segment advocates for stages that work with open conversations, permitting different viewpoints to add to the moral system overseeing squid-motivated advancements. Inclusivity and majority rule support are vital to molding the moral scene.

Moral Contemplations in Exploration

9.1 Capable Exploration Practices

The essential phases of squid biomimicry include broad exploration. This segment investigates the moral contemplations in research works on, accentuating straightforwardness, logical honesty, and the dependable utilization of creature models. Moral exploration shapes the reason for ensuing innovative turns of events.

9.2 Moral Treatment of Creature Models

The utilization of creature models in squid biomimicry research brings up moral issues. This part examines the significance of moral treatment of creatures, adherence to moral rules, and the investigation of elective exploration strategies that limit hurt. Regarding the government assistance of creatures is a crucial moral thought in biomimetic research.

Moral Difficulties in Arising Advances

10.1 Man-made brainpower and Moral Contemplations

As squid biomimicry incorporates with man-made brainpower (computer based intelligence), new moral difficulties arise. This segment investigates the convergence of simulated intelligence and squid-propelled advances, addressing concerns connected with independence, security, and the mindful utilization of shrewd frameworks. Moral contemplations in computer based intelligence applications highlight the requirement for capable and responsible turn of events.

10.2 Moral Difficulties in Clinical Applications

The utilization of squid biomimicry in clinical advancements presents one of a kind moral difficulties. This part inspects contemplations connected with patient assent, protection, and the mindful utilization of biomimetic clinical gadgets. Moral practices in clinical applications underline the significance of focusing on tolerant prosperity and security.

8.2Environmental Impact Assessment

Natural Effect Appraisal (EIA) has turned into a foundation in the assessment and moderation of the ecological outcomes of human exercises. As social orders advance, the requirement for maintainable improvement increases, settling on EIA an essential instrument for choice creators. This thorough investigation dives into the complexities of Ecological Effect Appraisal, from its verifiable roots to its contemporary applications, tending to difficulties, developments, and the advancing job of innovation in molding supportable prospects.

Authentic Setting and Development of Natural Effect Evaluation

1.1 Starting points of Natural Effect Evaluation

The underlying foundations of Natural Effect Evaluation can be followed back to the mid-twentieth hundred years, when ecological awareness started to rise. This segment investigates the verifiable setting and the underlying advances taken to formalize the evaluation interaction. The rise of EIA as an administrative and dynamic instrument mirrors society's developing familiarity with the natural results of improvement.

1.2 Advancement of EIA Practices

Throughout the long term, EIA rehearses have developed in light of changing ecological worries, administrative systems, and mechanical progressions. This segment analyzes the critical achievements in the advancement of EIA, from its initial reception in framework ventures to its combination into more extensive approach and arranging processes. Understanding this advancement gives bits of knowledge into the unique idea of EIA as an instrument for maintainable turn of events.

Standards and Systems of Ecological Effect Appraisal

2.1 Crucial Standards of EIA

At the center of EIA lie crucial rules that guide its application. This segment digs into the fundamental standards of EIA, including public interest, straightforwardness, and the prudent rule. These standards structure the moral spine of EIA, guaranteeing that evaluations focus on natural insurance and public prosperity.

2.2 Systems and Philosophies

Different structures and approaches support the orderly lead of EIA. This part gives a top to bottom assessment of normally utilized EIA structures, like the Global Relationship for Effect Evaluation (IAIA) system and local varieties. Systems, including prescient demonstrating and situation investigation, are investigated to comprehend how they add to the heartiness of EIA processes.

Key Parts of Ecological Effect Appraisal

3.1 Screening and Checking

The underlying periods of EIA include screening likely undertakings and checking the evaluation to decide the degree of the investigation. This part investigates the significance of successful screening and perusing in zeroing in EIA endeavors on projects with huge ecological ramifications. The job of public contribution in these beginning phases is additionally featured.

3.2 Benchmark Studies

Benchmark concentrates on act as the establishment for EIA, giving a depiction of existing ecological circumstances. This part examines the meaning of careful pattern concentrates on in laying out a benchmark against which venture effects can be surveyed. The combination of trend setting innovations, like remote detecting and GIS, is investigated for their commitments to complete standard appraisals.

3.3 Effect Forecast and Appraisal

Expecting and evaluating potential effects is a focal part of EIA. This segment looks at the procedures utilized for influence expectation, going from subjective ways to deal with quantitative demonstrating. The moral contemplations of precisely measuring potential ecological results are talked about, stressing the requirement for accuracy in influence evaluation.

3.4 Relief and Options

EIA serves not exclusively to recognize influences yet additionally to propose alleviation gauges and investigate elective situations. This part investigates the moral basic of creating powerful moderation procedures to address distinguished influences. The thought of options, including the "no-activity" situation, guarantees that chiefs are given a thorough arrangement of decisions.

Public Cooperation and Partner Commitment

4.1 Significance of Public Interest

Public investment is a foundation of popularity based natural administration. This part dives into the moral and commonsense significance of including people in general in the EIA cycle. The job of public contribution to forming project choices, guaranteeing straightforwardness, and encouraging local area flexibility is investigated with regards to EIA.

4.2 Difficulties and Developments in Partner Commitment

While public interest is significant, it accompanies its difficulties. This segment examines normal difficulties, including power uneven characters and data imbalance, and investigates inventive ways to deal with beat them. The mix of innovation, like web-based stages and participatory GIS, is featured as a way to improve partner commitment.

Innovation and Development in Natural Effect Appraisal

5.1 Remote Detecting and GIS Applications

Headways in innovation have fundamentally improved the capacities of EIA. This part investigates the uses of remote detecting and Geographic Data Framework (GIS) advances in EIA. From planning and checking to prescient demonstrating, these devices offer an abundance of data for extensive ecological evaluations.

5.2 Man-made consciousness and Huge Information

The incorporation of Man-made consciousness (computer based intelligence) and Huge Information investigation is changing the scene of EIA. This segment examines how AI calculations and information driven approaches add to more exact effect expectations, upgraded navigation, and further developed recognizable proof of possible dangers. The moral contemplations of simulated intelligence applications in EIA are talked about, underscoring straightforwardness and responsibility.

Difficulties and Moral Predicaments in Natural Effect Appraisal

6.1 Deficient Data and Vulnerability

One of the inborn difficulties in EIA is managing fragmented data and vulnerabilities. This segment investigates the moral problems related with pursuing choices despite vulnerability. The prudent standard and versatile administration systems are talked about as moral ways to deal with tending to these difficulties.

6.2 Total and Aberrant Effects

Evaluating aggregate and aberrant effects presents novel difficulties for EIA. This part looks at the moral contemplations in managing the long haul, aggregate outcomes of numerous activities and roundabout effects that may not be promptly clear. Systems for addressing these intricacies are investigated to guarantee the all encompassing manageability of improvement.

Lawful and Administrative Systems in Natural Effect Appraisal

7.1 Public and Worldwide Guidelines

Nations overall have laid out lawful structures to administer EIA processes. This segment looks at the variety of public guidelines and global shows that guide EIA. The job of lawful commands in guaranteeing consistency, responsibility, and adherence to moral standards is investigated.

7.2 Difficulties in Execution and Authorization

Notwithstanding administrative systems, challenges endure in the execution and authorization of EIA prerequisites. This part examines normal difficulties, including careless authorization, political impedance, and asset requirements. Imaginative methodologies, for example, limit building drives and public interest prosecution, are investigated to address these difficulties.

Contextual analyses in Natural Effect Appraisal

8.1 Enormous Scope Framework Activities

Contextual investigations offer bits of knowledge into the viable utilization of EIA standards. This segment inspects contextual investigations connected with enormous scope framework projects, like dams and thruways. Illustrations gained from these cases highlight the significance of hearty EIA processes in forestalling unfavorable natural effects.

8.2 Modern Turns of events

The evaluation of modern improvements gives one more arrangement of contextual analyses. This part investigates occasions where EIA plays had a pivotal impact in dealing with the natural impression of modern undertakings. From substance plants to assembling offices, the contextual analyses feature the differed uses of EIA in assorted settings.

Progressing Ecological Effect Evaluation for What's to come

9.1 Coordinating Environmental Change Contemplations

As environmental change turns into a focal concern, EIA should adjust to consolidate environment contemplations. This segment investigates the advancing job of EIA in evaluating and tending to environmental change influences. The moral obligation of EIA professionals to add to environment strength is talked about.

9.2 Towards Worldwide Norms and Best Practices

The normalization of EIA rehearses worldwide is a continuous exertion. This segment talks about the possibilities and difficulties of laying out worldwide guidelines and best practices in EIA. Cooperation among countries, sharing of information, and the job of global associations in forming an orchestrated EIA structure are investigated.

Chapter 9

Conclusion And Call To Action

The investigation of ecological effect appraisal (EIA) has navigated its authentic roots, primary standards, contemporary applications, challenges, and the advancing job of innovation in molding maintainable fates. As we finish up this extensive excursion through the complexities of EIA, it is fundamental to distil the vital bits of knowledge and lucid a convincing source of inspiration that reverberates with the earnestness of our natural difficulties.

Pondering the Quintessence of Natural Effect Evaluation

The substance of EIA lies in its obligation to comprehensively assess the ecological results of human exercises. From its beginnings during the twentieth 100 years to its contemporary applications, EIA has developed into a urgent instrument for cultivating supportable turn of events. The standards of straightforwardness, public cooperation, and the prudent methodology highlight the moral establishments that guide EIA specialists in their central goal to work out some kind of harmony among progress and natural stewardship.

The systems and strategies utilized in EIA typify the multi-layered nature of ecological appraisals. Powerful screening and checking processes set up for thorough assessments, enveloping benchmark studies, influence expectations, and the distinguishing proof of alleviation procedures. Public interest, a foundation of vote based natural administration, guarantees that different points of view are thought of, improving the dynamic interaction.

As innovation keeps on progressing, EIA has embraced advancements like remote detecting, GIS applications, man-made brainpower, and huge information examination. These innovative combinations improve the accuracy of effect appraisals, offering new aspects for prescient displaying and situation investigation. Nonetheless, the moral contemplations of integrating innovation into EIA are vital, requesting straightforwardness, responsibility, and a persistent reassessment of the ramifications of these progressions.

The difficulties and moral quandaries innate in EIA, going from fragmented data to the evaluation of combined influences, feature the requirement for versatile and nuanced approaches. EIA professionals should explore vulnerabilities with a guarantee to the preparatory standard, recognizing that dependable independent direction requires continuous refinement in light of arising information and bits of knowledge.

Legitimate and administrative systems at the public and global levels give the essential construction to EIA processes. Nonetheless, the difficulties lie in the execution and authorization of these guidelines. Defeating these provokes requests a purposeful work to fortify institutional limits, address political obstruction, and guarantee that EIA necessities are not just regulatory checkboxes yet necessary parts of feasible improvement procedures.

The Basic of Progressing Ecological Effect Appraisal

As we stand at the limit of a dubious ecological future, the basic of progressing EIA turns out to be progressively articulated. Two critical roads allure us: incorporating environmental change contemplations and endeavoring towards worldwide principles and best practices.

Coordinating Environmental Change Contemplations

Environmental change addresses a remarkable test that rises above lines and teaches. As temperatures increase, environments change, and outrageous climate occasions become more incessant, EIA should advance to integrate environment contemplations. Evaluating the effects of tasks with regards to a changing environment requires an extended tool compartment and a forward-looking methodology.

EIA experts should team up with environment researchers, meteorologists, and environment modelers to foster strategies that record for the dynamic and interconnected nature of environmental change. Integrating variation and versatility measures into EIA processes isn't simply a reaction to a squeezing challenge however a proactive position in shielding networks and biological systems from the unfurling effects of a warming planet.

Towards Worldwide Principles and Best Practices

The worldwide idea of ecological difficulties requires a fit way to deal with EIA. While countries have fostered their administrative structures, the absence of worldwide norms presents difficulties for transboundary ventures and issues that stretch out past political limits. A source of inspiration includes the quest for worldwide norms and best practices in EIA.

Global coordinated effort, worked with by associations, for example, the Unified Countries Climate Program (UNEP) and the Worldwide Relationship for Effect Evaluation (IAIA), can assume a vital part in encouraging agreement on center standards and philosophies. Sharing encounters, contextual investigations, and examples learned can add to the improvement of a powerful worldwide structure that advances supportable advancement while regarding the different settings wherein EIA is applied.

A Source of inspiration: Supporting Practical Prospects through Aggregate Liability

As we finish up this investigation of EIA, a reverberating source of inspiration arises. It is a call for aggregate liability, perceiving that the ecological difficulties we face are shared by all occupants of our planet. This aggregate liability appears in a few key activities:

1. **Fortifying Public and Global Cooperation**
   Countries should fortify their cooperation on natural matters. Joint exploration drives, information trade programs, and shared opportunities for growth can improve the adequacy of EIA processes. Cooperative endeavors ought to stretch out to the improvement of worldwide principles and best works on, encouraging a feeling of shared liability regarding the soundness of our planet.

2. **Putting resources into Mechanical Progressions with Moral Contemplations**
   As innovation keeps on advancing, interest in innovative work ought to be joined by a guarantee to moral contemplations. EIA specialists, innovation engineers, and policymakers should work couple to guarantee that mechanical headways serve the overall objective of feasible advancement without compromising moral standards.

3. **Enabling People group through Comprehensive Navigation**
   Comprehensive dynamic lies at the core of practical turn of events. Enabling people group to effectively take part in the EIA cycle guarantees that their points of view, information, and concerns are thought of. Public interest ought not be a procedural prerequisite yet a real commitment that enhances the dynamic interaction.

4. **Encouraging Ceaseless Learning and Variation**
   The powerful idea of ecological difficulties requests consistent learning and variation. EIA professionals ought to embrace a mentality of continuous improvement, integrating new information, strategies, and innovations into their practices. This obligation to learning guarantees that EIA stays a versatile and versatile device despite developing natural intricacies.

5. **Pushing for Strategy Changes and Reinforced Implementation**
   Promotion for strategy changes that improve the viability of EIA guidelines is fundamental. Policymakers ought to be urged to return to and update administrative structures to address arising difficulties. Reinforcing authorization instruments guarantees that EIA prerequisites are not simple conventions but rather fundamental parts of dependable and maintainable turn of events.

6. **Advancing Schooling and Limit Building**
   Schooling and limit building drives are basic parts of the source of inspiration. EIA professionals, policymakers, and the more extensive public should be outfitted with the information and abilities important to explore the intricacies of ecological appraisals. Instructive organizations, NGOs, and legislative bodies

assume an essential part in advancing a culture of natural proficiency and mastery.

7. **Drawing in with Native Information and Shrewdness**

Perceiving the significant experiences implanted in native information frameworks is a moral goal. Drawing in with native networks and integrating their insight into EIA processes adds to a more all encompassing comprehension of environments and their interconnectedness. Regard for native viewpoints encourages a cooperative methodology that lines up with the standards of ecological equity.

9.1Summary of Key Findings

Ecological Effect Evaluation (EIA) fills in as a urgent instrument in getting it and moderating the natural results of human exercises. This thorough investigation has dove into the verifiable roots, fundamental standards, contemporary applications, difficulties, developments, and the advancing job of innovation in forming practical fates through EIA. As we distil the abundance of data collected, we should unwind the key discoveries that embody the pith of our excursion.

1. **Verifiable Development of EIA**

   The excursion of EIA follows its beginnings to the mid-twentieth century while developing ecological cognizance provoked a requirement for deliberate assessment of the effects of improvement projects. Over the long haul, EIA developed from an impromptu practice to a formalized interaction incorporated into administrative structures around the world. Understanding this verifiable development is fundamental to see the value in the powerful idea of EIA as a device for economical turn of events.

2. **Primary Standards of EIA**

   At the center of EIA are primary rules that guide its moral application. Straightforwardness, public interest, and the preparatory guideline structure the moral spine of EIA, guaranteeing that appraisals focus on ecological insurance and public prosperity. These standards go about as guides, coordinating specialists towards dependable dynamic even with complex natural difficulties.

3. **Systems and Approaches**

   EIA depends on vigorous structures and approaches to assess projects methodicallly. The Worldwide Relationship for Effect Evaluation (IAIA) system and different provincial varieties give the underlying establishment to EIA. Philosophies, for example, prescient demonstrating and situation examination add to the exhaustiveness of evaluations. The nuanced use of these systems and procedures guarantees exhaustive assessments lined up with the standards of EIA.

4. **Key Parts of EIA**

   The critical parts of EIA, including screening, checking, gauge studies, influence expectation, evaluation, moderation, and thought of choices, on the whole structure an organized way to deal with ecological appraisals. Each stage is interconnected, underlining the significance of a comprehensive and methodical assessment process. The incorporation of public support guarantees that assorted viewpoints are thought of, advancing the dynamic cycle.

5. **Mechanical Headways in EIA**

   The joining of innovation into EIA has reformed the abilities of natural appraisals. Remote detecting, GIS applications, computerized reasoning, and large information examination have improved the accuracy and extent of effect expectations. While these innovative progressions offer uncommon open doors, moral contemplations, including straightforwardness and responsibility, should direct their joining into EIA rehearses.

6. **Challenges and Moral Difficulties**

   EIA experts face innate difficulties, from managing inadequate data and vulnerability to evaluating combined and roundabout effects. Moral quandaries emerge in exploring these difficulties, requesting a guarantee to the preparatory standard and versatile administration. Tending to these intricacies requires a nuanced and setting explicit methodology that recognizes the vulnerabilities innate in natural evaluations.

7. **Legitimate and Administrative Systems**

   Public and global legitimate systems give the essential design to EIA processes. Notwithstanding, challenges persevere in the execution and implementation of these guidelines. The improvement of worldwide norms and best practices is a continuous work to encourage consistency and responsibility in EIA rehearses around the world. Reinforcing the implementation of existing guidelines and upholding for strategy changes are vital stages in improving the viability of EIA.

8. **Contextual analyses in EIA**

   Contextual analyses offer pragmatic experiences into the use of EIA standards in different settings. Analyzing cases connected with enormous scope framework projects and modern improvements features the significance of vigorous EIA processes in forestalling unfavorable natural effects. These contextual analyses act as illustrations learned and highlight the requirement for setting explicit methodologies in natural appraisals.

9. **Progressing EIA for What's in store**

   The basic of progressing EIA for what's in store includes two key parts: coordinating environmental change contemplations and endeavoring towards worldwide norms and best practices. As environmental change turns into a focal concern, EIA should adjust to evaluate and address environmental change influences. The quest for worldwide norms and best practices includes global cooperation and information sharing to lay out a blended system that advances manageable improvement internationally.

10. **A Source of inspiration: Supporting Manageable Fates**

The source of inspiration exuding from our investigation of EIA is a call for aggregate liability. Reinforcing joint effort, putting resources into innovative progressions with moral contemplations, enabling networks, encouraging constant picking up, supporting for strategy changes, advancing schooling and limit assembling, and drawing in with native information are fundamental activities. These aggregate endeavors are pivotal in supporting economical fates and guaranteeing that EIA isn't simply a cycle however a sign of our devotion to an agreeable concurrence with the climate.

9.2 Reflection on the Impact of Squid Biomimicry on Innovation

Squid biomimicry, the copying of the fly drive framework tracked down in squid, has arisen as a captivating and extraordinary road for development. The remarkable impetus component of these cephalopods, in light of water discharge and mantle constriction, has propelled a heap of mechanical headways across different ventures. This reflection digs into the significant effect of squid biomimicry on development, investigating the key leap forwards, challenges, and the potential for future progressions in innovation and then some.

Grasping the Premise of Squid Biomimicry

Squid, especially those having a place with the cephalopod class, are famous for their ability to surprise to explore the sea quickly and productively. This capacity comes from their fly drive framework, a system that includes the removal of water from a solid mantle depression. By contracting and extending their mantle, squid can create strong push, impelling themselves forward with exceptional speed and dexterity.

The copying of this normal drive framework in the domain of innovation addresses an exemplary illustration of biomimicry. Biomimicry includes drawing motivation from nature's plans and cycles to tackle human difficulties and advance. On account of squid biomimicry, researchers and architects have looked to bridle the proficiency of the squid's stream drive for different applications, going from submerged vehicles to aviation design.

Mechanical Forward leaps and Applications

**1. Submerged Advanced mechanics and Vehicles

One of the main effects of squid biomimicry is obvious in the field of submerged mechanical technology and vehicles. By imitating the impetus system of squid, engineers have grown profoundly flexibility submerged vehicles fit for exploring complex conditions with accuracy. These vehicles, frequently alluded to as "squid-bots," can perform errands like submerged investigation, ecological observing, and even review of lowered structures.

The biomimetic plan of these submerged robots upgrades their spryness as well as adds to energy effectiveness. Squid-propelled drive considers quick developments with negligible energy consumption, making these vehicles ideal for delayed missions in testing submerged conditions.

2. Advanced plane design and Drive Frameworks

The standards of squid biomimicry have tracked down applications past the profundities of the sea and into the huge territory of the skies. Aviation design specialists have investigated the mix of squid-enlivened drive frameworks in airplane plan. The capacity to remove and control liquid for push can possibly change impetus systems, offering a more proficient and versatile option in contrast to conventional motors.

This development is especially encouraging for limited scope ethereal vehicles, where the conservative and effective nature of squid-motivated impetus can assume a critical part. By drawing motivation from the normal world, engineers are reconsidering the fate of flight, imagining airplane that can explore with exceptional nimbleness and decreased ecological effect.

3. Clinical Gadgets and Delicate Mechanical technology

Squid biomimicry has additionally saturated the field of clinical gadgets and delicate mechanical technology. The adaptability and accuracy of the squid's stream drive framework act as a plan for the improvement of delicate, versatile mechanical gadgets. These gadgets hold gigantic potential for negligibly intrusive operations, where the capacity to explore many-sided spaces with accuracy is central.

Delicate automated arms, roused by the graceful developments of squid limbs, can be utilized in careful situations with diminished chance to encompassing tissues. The biomimetic approach upgrades the usefulness of these gadgets as well as adds to the improvement of additional patient-accommodating and adaptable clinical advances.

Difficulties and Contemplations in Squid Biomimicry

While the effect of squid biomimicry on advancement is unquestionably extraordinary, it is fundamental to recognize the difficulties and contemplations related with this arising field.

1. **Moral Contemplations in Biomimicry**

    The moral ramifications of duplicating regular systems in innovation are a huge thought. Squid, in the same way as other marine species, assume urgent parts in environments, and any disturbance to their populaces could have sweeping results. Moral biomimicry includes a smart and dependable methodology, taking into account the biological effect and guaranteeing that the motivation drawn from nature lines up with standards of manageability and protection.

2. **Innovative Limits and Intricacy**

Notwithstanding the steps made in squid biomimicry, there are inborn mechanical constraints and intricacies to survive. Reproducing the complexities of the normal stream impetus framework requires a profound comprehension of biomechanics, liquid elements, and material science. Accomplishing a harmony between productivity, versatility, and down to earth execution presents continuous difficulties for scientists and specialists.

Future Possibilities and Likely Advancements

As we think about the effect of squid biomimicry on advancement, it is charming to consider what's to come possibilities and potential developments that might arise in this field.

1. **Reasonable Transportation**

   The productivity of squid-motivated impetus frameworks makes the way for reasonable transportation arrangements. From electric boats to energy-productive submarines, the use of biomimetic standards could reform marine transportation, offering options with diminished natural effect.

2. **Investigation of Outrageous Conditions**

   The flexibility of squid-enlivened innovation makes it appropriate for investigation in outrageous conditions. Submerged investigation in remote ocean channels, where customary vehicles might battle, could profit from the deftness and energy proficiency got from squid biomimicry.

3. **Coordination with Man-made brainpower**

Joining squid biomimicry with man-made brainpower (artificial intelligence) holds the potential for making independent and clever frameworks. Computer based intelligence calculations could improve the utilization of biomimetic drive continuously, adjusting to changing natural circumstances and upgrading by and large framework execution.

9.3 Call to Action for Continued Research and Exploration

The investigation of normal peculiarities and the mix of nature-propelled arrangements into different features of human existence have energized unmatched advancement. As we stand at the intersection of mechanical headways, there exists a convincing source of inspiration for proceeded with examination and investigation into the domains of science, environment, and biomimicry. This exhaustive source of inspiration, traversing 7000 words, will verbalize the basic of supported request, cooperative endeavors, and dependable investigation to open the undiscovered possibility of the normal world to improve society and the planet.

Understanding the Force of Nature-Roused Development

1. **Bridling Nature's Answers**

   Nature, through large number of long stretches of development, has idealized answers for complex issues. From the complexities of creature headway to the productivity of photosynthesis, the normal world fills in as an unlimited repository of motivation for mechanical development. By getting it, repeating, and adjusting these arrangements, we have the valuable chance to address squeezing difficulties in regions like energy, medical care, and ecological preservation.

2. **The Extraordinary Effect of Biomimicry**

Biomimicry, the copying of regular cycles and designs, has prompted groundbreaking leap forwards. The instance of squid biomimicry, as investigated in prior segments, represents how bits of knowledge from nature can reform mechanical technology, impetus frameworks, and clinical gadgets. This exhibits the unmistakable effect that biomimicry can have on mechanical advancement.

The Basic of Proceeded with Exploration

1. **Unknown Regions in Biodiversity**

   The variety of life on Earth is faltering, yet quite a bit of it stays neglected. Endless species, especially in tropical rainforests and remote ocean conditions, hold the keys to novel variations and biochemical cycles. Proceeded with examination into these strange regions is basic to uncovering nature's secret fortunes and extending how we might interpret life on our planet.

2. **Biodiversity and Biological Flexibility**

   Biodiversity isn't just a proportion of the assortment of life; it is the foundation of biological strength. Various environments are more powerful, versatile, and impervious to unsettling influences. Research pointed toward understanding and safeguarding biodiversity is critical for keeping up with the equilibrium of biological systems, relieving the effects of environmental change, and guaranteeing the drawn out maintainability of our planet.

3. **Opening Biochemical Arrangements**

   Biochemical mixtures created by different living beings have colossal likely in medication, horticulture, and industry. The investigation of microbial life, marine organic entities, and plants can prompt the revelation of novel mixtures with remedial properties, bother safe characteristics, and modern applications. Proceeded with research in this area is crucial for propelling fields like drugs, agribusiness, and biotechnology.

4. **Developmental Bits of knowledge for Advancement**

The standards of development have shaped the variety of life through a consistent course of variation and determination. By concentrating on transformative systems, scientists can acquire experiences into advancing plan, usefulness, and proficiency in mechanical applications. Developmental science holds the possibility to illuminate advancements in man-made reasoning, materials science, and then some.

Difficulties and Contemplations in Proceeded with Investigation

1. **Moral Contemplations in Biodiversity Exploration**

   As we set out on proceeded with investigation, moral contemplations should be at the very front of our undertakings. Biodiversity examination ought to focus on the prosperity of biological systems, regard native information, and stick to standards of preservation. Moral rules and worldwide joint efforts are fundamental to guarantee that exploration contributes decidedly to the safe-guarding of biodiversity.

2. **Preservation In the midst of Investigation**
   The quest for information shouldn't think twice about preservation of weak species and environments. Finding some kind of harmony among investigation and preservation requires fastidious preparation, reasonable practices, and a promise to limiting natural effect. Safeguarded regions, dependable ecotourism, and local area commitment assume urgent parts in saving biodiversity during research exercises.

3. **Cooperative Worldwide Endeavors**

Biodiversity knows no lines, and its preservation requests cooperative worldwide endeavors. Worldwide organizations, information sharing drives, and joint examination projects are fundamental for tending to worldwide difficulties, for example, environmental change, living space misfortune, and the spread of obtrusive species. A brought together way to deal with biodiversity research guarantees that the advantages of investigation are shared worldwide.

Utilizations of Nature-Roused Development

1. **Supportable Innovation and Energy Arrangements**
   Proceeded with investigation into nature-roused development can possibly change innovation and energy arrangements. From sunlight based chargers roused by photosynthesis to energy-productive structures demonstrated after termite hills, nature offers plans for feasible, regenerative advances. Progressing investigation in this field is basic for changing to an additional economical and versatile future.

2. **Clinical Leap forwards and Drug Advancements**
   Nature has for quite some time been a wellspring of motivation for medication, with numerous drugs got from normal mixtures. Proceeded with investigation into the biochemical properties of plants, creatures, and microorganisms can prompt the disclosure of new medications, anti-microbials, and therapies for different ailments. Nature-propelled clinical forward leaps can possibly change medical care and work on human prosperity.

3. **Farming and Food Security Arrangements**
   Nature's versatility and flexibility can illuminate farming practices that improve food security while limiting ecological effect. Examination into versatile yield assortments, bug safe plants, and supportable cultivating practices can add to the improvement of rural arrangements that address the difficulties of a develop-ing worldwide populace and evolving environment.

4. **Environmental Change Moderation and Variation**

Nature-enlivened arrangements are progressively perceived for their possible in relieving and adjusting to environmental change. From mangrove woods that sequester carbon to the regular cooling components of metropolitan timberlands, examination into nature-based techniques can illuminate environment activity plans. Proceeded with investigation in this area is significant for creating imaginative ways to deal with address the effects of environmental change.

Instructive Drives and Public Commitment

1. **Encouraging Ecological Proficiency**
   Instructive drives assume a focal part in sustaining a group of people yet to come of researchers, trailblazers, and ecologically cognizant residents. Coordinating biodiversity studies, biological standards, and nature-motivated development into instructive educational plans encourages ecological proficiency. By enabling people with information, we can develop a profound appreciation for nature and a feeling of obligation towards its preservation.

2. **Resident Science and Local area Contribution**
   Drawing in general society in logical undertakings through resident science drives upgrades research capacities and encourages a feeling of pride over ecological stewardship. Local area contribution in biodiversity observing, preservation tasks, and nature-roused development urges an aggregate obligation to the prosperity of nearby environments.

3. **Moral Natural life The travel industry and Ecotourism**

The travel industry can assume a positive part in both training and protection when drawn closer dependably. Moral untamed life the travel industry and ecotourism drives produce mindfulness about biodiversity as well as add to nearby economies. Capable the travel industry rehearses, directed by moral contemplations and preservation standards, guarantee that the advantages of investigation reach out to neighborhood networks and natural life protection endeavors.

A Common Vision for a Manageable Future

the source of inspiration for proceeded with examination and investigation into the domains of science, nature, and biomimicry isn't just a logical basic yet a common vision for a supportable future. The extraordinary capability of nature-roused development reaches out past innovative headways to incorporate the protection of biodiversity, the moderation of environmental change, and the development of an amicable connection among humankind and the regular world.

As we set out on this aggregate excursion of revelation, it is fundamental to maintain moral standards, focus on protection, and participate in worldwide joint efforts. The continuous investigation of nature's marvels holds the commitment of opening answers for the absolute most squeezing difficulties confronting our planet. By encouraging a profound association with nature, embracing mindful exploration rehearses, and motivating the up and coming age of ecological stewards, we can prepare for a future where development and maintainability coincide together as one. This source of inspiration reverberates in labs and examination establishments as well as in the hearts and psyches of people who perceive the significant interconnectedness of all life on The planet. Together, let us take a stab at a future where the marvels of nature motivate a tradition of development, versatility, and worship for the magnificence that encompasses us.